AN INVITATION TO BIBLICAL POETRY

ESSENTIALS OF BIBLICAL STUDIES

Series Editor
Patricia K. Tull, Louisville Presbyterian Theological Seminary

AN INVITATION TO BIBLICAL POETRY
Elaine T. James

ANCIENT ISRAEL'S NEIGHBORS
Brian R. Doak

SIN IN THE NEW TESTAMENT
Jeffrey Siker

READING HEBREW BIBLE NARRATIVES
J. Andrew Dearman

THE HISTORY OF BRONZE AND IRON AGE ISRAEL
Victor H. Matthews

NEW TESTAMENT CHRISTIANITY IN THE ROMAN WORLD
Harry O. Maier

WOMEN IN THE NEW TESTAMENT WORLD
Susan E. Hylen

An Invitation to Biblical Poetry

ELAINE T. JAMES

OXFORD
UNIVERSITY PRESS

OXFORD
UNIVERSITY PRESS

Oxford University Press is a department of the University of Oxford. It furthers
the University's objective of excellence in research, scholarship, and education
by publishing worldwide. Oxford is a registered trade mark of Oxford University
Press in the UK and certain other countries.

Published in the United States of America by Oxford University Press
198 Madison Avenue, New York, NY 10016, United States of America.

Library of Congress Control Number: 2021943350
ISBN 978–0–19–066493–0 (pbk.)
ISBN 978–0–19–066492–3 (hbk.)

DOI: 10.1093/oso/9780190664923.001.0001

Paperback printed by Marquis, Canada
Hardback printed by Bridgeport National Bindery, Inc., United States of America

*There is always something stupid about turning poetry into a prose
that is supposed to explain the meaning of the poetry.*

—JOHN DEWEY

If the Psalms aren't poetry, they're useless.

—ALICIA SUSKIN OSTRIKER

CONTENTS

ACKNOWLEDGMENTS

In writing this book for students and general readers, my articulations of ideas about poetry have been profoundly shaped by the wisdom of others, and my debts are far greater than I can acknowledge. My first words, therefore, go to the many poets and scholars whose work I have learned from and absorbed over so many years that their thinking has become my thinking. To all the people I have learned from and have subsequently forgotten that I have learned from: I'm sorry, and thank you.

My first traceable debt is to my parents: Norman James, who read me countless nursery rhymes as a child and who has always been a maker of beautiful things; and Theresa James, who is a reader and writer of poetry, and whose copy of John Donne's poems I borrowed sometime in the 1990s and only now confess to still harboring. I am grateful to many poets I have known and loved, especially Sarah Olson, who generously read and critiqued at every stage. Thanks are due to the Coattails, especially Carmen Goetschius, David Hallgren, Kristin Hallgren, Andrea Haughton Kladder, and Ben Lattimer. Thanks are forever due to Luis Rivera-Pagan, who inspired our first meeting and who agreed to join us if we served wine.

To colleagues who read chapters and discussed the ideas of this book with me, I express my deepest thanks. At the top of this list is Blake Couey, who has been a peerless collaborator and the dearest friend. I have benefited from his generosity in scholarly dialogue for many years, and it is my intention to do so for many more. I am also enormously indebted to Sean Burt for his invigorating co-conspiracy and thoughtful, creative comments on this work. With profound gratitude for their generosities of time, conversation, reading, and friendship, I also thank Simeon Chavel, Stephanie Cohen, Heath Dewrell, Rhiannon Graybill, Nyasha Junior, Amy Levad, Hanne Loeland Levinson, Abigail Pelham, Daniel Pioske, Jeremy Schipper, and Anne Stewart. Thank you to Leslie Virnelson and Andrew Garbarino for reading with a keen eye. Thank you to the wonderful scholars of the Twin Cities Bible Colloquium, whose friendship and cheerful collaboration warmed many Minnesota days, especially Marian Broida, Corrine Carvalho, Dean Erickson, Ryan Higgins, Bernard Levinson, Anna Marsh, Meredith Nyberg, Maggie Odell, David Penchansky, and Ronald Troxel. Thank you to my colleagues at St. Catherine University, where I began this work, especially Hella Cohen, Francine Conley, Karen Guth, Cecilia Konchar-Farr, and Rachel Neiwert, for their conviviality and feminist brilliance. To my colleagues at Princeton Theological Seminary, especially the warm community in and around the department of Old Testament, including Elizabeth Bloch-Smith, Jacqueline Lapsley, Dennis Olson, Brian Rainey, and Mark Smith: I am honored to work beside you and could not imagine a happier place in which to conclude this work.

I am grateful to the editorial team at Oxford University Press, especially Steve Wiggins. Patricia Tull has been a thoughtful and thorough editor who pressed me with patience and skill to clearer articulations of my ideas. Thanks to the anonymous reviewers of this manuscript, both for their critical feedback, which shaped the work in development and revision, and for their forbearance of those places where I chose a different path.

Above all, I am grateful to my family. To my children, Hank and Forest, thank you for the constant reminder of poetry's power and sheer, nonsensical delight. To my partner in all things, Nathaniel Van Yperen: Thank you for joining me at readings, for endless conversation and encouragement, and for your cheerful capacity to make in your own busy life a spacious and kindly habitat for other creatures, especially me. Thank you for the daily reminder that our life is a work of art.

Ultimate thanks go to Chip Dobbs-Allsopp, my excellent teacher, dear colleague, and friend. His infectious enthusiasm initially brought me to the study of biblical Hebrew poetry and his unflagging encouragement led me to believe that I could write such a book. This handbook owes an unmeasurable debt to his thinking, which will be obvious to anyone who knows his work. He also has the uncommon generosity of spirit to encourage students and colleagues to develop their own voices, even in departures from his own thought. (So, for the idiosyncrasies of this work, I take full responsibility.) I am also profoundly grateful to Leslie Dobbs-Allsopp, for her wisdom and kindness over now many years. Their endlessly warm hospitality and friendship also serve as an invitation to practical, interdisciplinary thinking. It would take a poem to express my thanks.

SERIES INTRODUCTION

The past three decades have seen an explosion of approaches to study of the Bible, as older exegetical methods have been joined by a variety of literary, anthropological, and social models. Interfaith collaboration has helped change the field, and the advent of more cultural diversity among biblical scholars in the West and around the world has broadened our reading and interpretation of the Bible. These changes have also fueled interest in Scripture's past: both the ancient Near Eastern and Mediterranean worlds out of which Scripture came and the millennia of premodern interpretation through which it traveled to our day. The explosion of information and perspectives is so vast that no one textbook can any longer address the many needs of seminaries and colleges where the Bible is studied.

In addition to these developments in the field itself are changes in the students. Traditionally the domain of seminaries, graduate schools, and college and university religion classes, now biblical study also takes place in a host of alternative venues. As lay leadership in local churches develops, nontraditional, weekend, and online preparatory classes have mushroomed. As seminaries in Africa, Asia, and Latin America grow, particular need for inexpensive, easily available materials is clear. As religious controversies over the Bible's origins and norms continue to dominate the airwaves, congregation members and even curious nonreligious folk seek reliable paths into particular topics. And teachers themselves continue to seek guidance in areas of the ever-expanding field of scriptural study with which they may be less than familiar.

A third wave of changes also makes this series timely: shifts in the publishing industry itself. Technologies and knowledge are shifting so rapidly that large books are out of date almost before they are in print. The internet and the growing popularity of e-books call for flexibility and accessibility in marketing and sales. If the days when one expert can sum up the field in a textbook are gone, also gone are the days when large, expensive multi-authored tomes are attractive to students, teachers, and other readers.

During my own years of seminary teaching, I have tried to find just the right book or books for just the right price, at just the right reading level for my students, with just enough information to orient them without drowning them in excess reading. For all the reasons stated above, this search was all too often less than successful. So I was excited to be asked to help Oxford University Press assemble a select crew of leading scholars to create a series that would respond to such classroom challenges. Essentials of Biblical Studies comprises freestanding, relatively brief, accessibly written books that provide orientation to the Bible's contents, its ancient contexts, its interpretive methods and history, and its themes and figures. Rather than a one-size-had-better-fit-all approach, these books may be mixed and matched to suit the objectives of a variety of classroom venues as well as the needs of individuals wishing to find their way into unfamiliar topics.

I am confident that our book authors will join me in returning enthusiastic thanks to the editorial staff at Oxford University Press for their support and guidance, especially Theo Calderara, who shepherded the project in its early days, and Dr. Steve Wiggins, who has been a most wise and steady partner in this work since joining OUP in 2013.

Introduction

An Art of Words

THIS BOOK IS AN INVITATION to biblical poetry, with students and general readers in mind. It is written with the conviction that people read poetry—even some of the most ancient poetry—because it offers meaningful experiences to readers. It speaks to us and it speaks for us, and it helps us frame crucial questions about our lives. My hope is that this book might both orient readers to the texts and enrich their experiences of reading them.

I write this introduction under conditions of social distancing resulting from the coronavirus outbreak in the spring of 2020. I mention this because I believe that the social circumstances of readers have an important bearing on their readings of texts. This is true for all readers of biblical poetry. This is true for me. In such circumstances, we cannot help but be reminded of our creatureliness and our fragility—both individually and communally. The human community is fragmented by isolation and shaken by devastating losses of all kinds.

This experience of generalized fear, alongside the anguish of suffering and the banality of isolation, is not a new experience in human history. One place we find traces of such experiences is in the arts. We make art not only in spite of our distress but also because of it. An ancient poem offers these words as an incantation

An Invitation to Biblical Poetry. Elaine T. James, Oxford University Press. © Oxford University Press 2022.
DOI: 10.1093/oso/9780190664923.003.0001

for protection. They echo with painful familiarity our current plight. Here are selected lines:

> Surely he (God) will deliver you
> from the snare of the fowler,
> from the ruinous plague . . .
> You will not fear the terror of night,
> the arrow that flies by day,
> the plague that stalks in darkness,
> the destruction that wastes at noon. . . .
> He will not let evil befall you,
> or disease draw near your tent. (Psalm 91:3, 5–6, 10)[1]

The description of the plague is wrenching: it cannot be seen but seems to stalk us everywhere, bringing with it "evil" and "destruction." The pestilence is compared to deadly arrows and a trap that might spring imminent death on the unsuspecting. The fact that it has been given poetic form renders this experience both timeless (we can read and identify with it millennia later) and, we might also say, beautiful. There is an arc to this description of danger that is not only harrowing but also aesthetic.

The aesthetic experience offered by this poem invites us to see ourselves in the poem the moment it opens with these mysterious words: "One who dwells in the secret of the Most High / who in the shadow of the Almighty spends the night" (Psalm 91:1). Who is the "one who dwells?" we might ask. "Is it me?" The next line draws the reader or hearer of this poem more fully in: "I say to the Lord, 'my refuge and my stronghold / my God, in whom I trust'" (Psalm 91:2). In the shift to "I" language in the second verse, the reader takes up the refuge that the first lines allude to. As I write this during shelter-in-place directives, these lines seem acutely attuned to such situations in which our vulnerability requires a haven. They offer a verbal canopy that evokes the protective divine presence for the one who hears or speaks them. For the ancients—whoever composed or sang this poem, and whoever might have written it down—this poem was necessary. And it is necessary, too, for those who memorized it (as many have done over the centuries) and for those who carried it with them, inscribed on some object, as a protective amulet (as many have also done over the centuries).[2] The poem offers a way to wrestle with a terror of unknown dimensions. It makes that experience of terror worthy of intense consideration. It also provides an experience of beauty that is itself a shelter for those who read it.

The poem's aesthetic sensibility is developed in a number of complex ways. I will draw attention to just a few of them here. As I noted, the first line's syntax is strange and open—it evokes the secrecy of shelter, and it gives us an image of the "shadow," of the Almighty, a place of refuge where one might "spend the night"— one of our most vulnerable needs—unharmed. The atmosphere is dark and threatening. We have an immediate sense of the hugeness of the deity, though not yet a full sense of the scope of God's presence. In verses 3–4, this will be more fully explored:

> Surely he (God) will deliver you
> from the snare of the fowler,
> from the ruinous plague.
> With his pinions he will cover you
> and under his wings you will take refuge. (Psalm 91:3–4)

The imagery becomes more vivid here and holds together more than one dimension of poetic language. The vulnerable person is now a hunted bird. This seems to be a metaphor for the plague in the next line. But the plague itself also operates as a metaphor, as the poem will go on to draw on imagery of military victory (Psalm 91:7–8) and of protection—perhaps spiritual protection—by divine beings (Psalm 91:11–12). In this way we can see the poem opening onto a multiplicity of meanings, inviting the reader to draw out metaphorical implications for themselves. It asks us to imagine what we need protection from. Even more remarkable,

God is envisioned as an enormous bird whose wings provide the shelter (the "shadow," v. 1) for the threatened speaker. This staging of divine presence engages the imagination in a way that a straightforward declarative like "God is my shelter" does not. In the poem, we are in a world where we are birds and God is a mother bird with protective wings. For ancient Israelites, this may have evoked the wings of the cherubim in the temple, hovering over the ark of the covenant. For contemporary and ancient audiences alike, the imagery is capable of evoking a whole realm of unpredictable associations and feelings. The poet will go on to convey the totalizing experience of fear through parallel lines: the threat stalks in day and night, in darkness and at noon (vv. 5–6). These parallels are not mere statements of fact; they are verbal figures that create the sense of being surrounded at every moment, with no possibility of escape. In this state of persistent threat, the plague is personified: it "stalks," giving it a sense of terrifying agency. In verse 13, the poem uses even more concrete imagery of wild creatures, this time to imagine divine victory: "On cobra and lion you will tread / you will trample the cub and the serpent" (Psalm 91:13). In ancient thought, wild beasts are often associated with forces of chaos that threaten to undo the order of the world. The poem lifts us out of the banality of living daily with fear and imagines a great victory of mythological proportions, in which the seemingly untamable wildness is conquered by a great intervention of divine power. This victory is secured by the words of divine assurance with which the poem ends. Here, the voicing shifts, and God speaks these promises of rescue:

> Because he loves me, I will rescue him.
> I will protect him because he knows my name.
> He will call me, and I will answer him.
> I will be with him in trouble.
> I will rescue him and I will honor him.
> With length of days I will satisfy him,
> and I will show him my deliverance. (Psalm 91:14–16)

The poem itself becomes a way to make the deliverance of God visible or discernible to one who lives in the unsettling experience of being afraid. In such ways, we begin to see how the poets of the Bible were making art with words.

As art, these poems do intellectual work. They are deeply engaged in the questions and problems of human experience. I emphasize this in part because the Bible is often popularly characterized as didactic literature—its purpose is instructional, it aims to teach, and therefore the goal of reading is to extract the correct "message." Biblical poetry *can* do these things, and some biblical poems are manifestly didactic (think, for example, of the many examples in the book of Proverbs). But to imagine that this is the only thing biblical poems do is needlessly limiting. As the example of Psalm 91 helps us see, the value of the poem is not only in our ability to reduce it to a digestible point of instruction. Rather, the poems are creating experiences that invite our deep consideration and participation. They are doing the kinds of work that art can do. Alva Noë, a contemporary philosopher, writes:

> Science and philosophy, to the extent that they concern themselves with art, tend to do so from on high. They seek to *explain* art, to treat art as a phenomenon to be analyzed. Maybe we've been overlooking the possibility that art can be our teacher, or at least our collaborator. Not because art is cryptoscience, but because it is its own manner of investigation and its own legitimate source of knowledge.[3]

Noë identifies here exactly the tendency one often encounters in readings of biblical poems—we want to "explain" them (and one can find many, many commentaries on biblical poems that do just that). Yet he also suggests a provocative possibility that might reorient our approach to these ancient texts. In describing art as "its own manner of investigation" *and* "its own legitimate source of knowledge," Noë elevates the contributions of the arts to humanistic inquiry. Poetry itself might be a source of knowledge, with its own unique ways of engaging the world and its own intellectual contributions. I am seeking here to broaden our sense of what is possible within biblical poems and to consider how they invite us to collaborate with them as they and we confront all the anguishing problems and perennial joys of human life. Because these problems and joys are so variable and diverse, we might expect that the poetry and aesthetics of the Bible will also be variable and diverse. They are.

This book offers a corrective to approaches to biblical poetry that see poems as primarily rhetorical. This is an unfortunate and naïve way to think about why literature is created or how it lives and retains power for later communities of readers. Verbal arts are not merely containers for a message that is supposed to have one specific, discernable rhetorical impact on an audience. While this is still a pervasive view of biblical poetry within the field of biblical studies, this view is too monolithic and expects of a poem too much tidiness, not to mention a level of historical specificity that is finer than our knowledge, which is often murky. To take the approach I advocate requires instead that we acknowledge how the arts operate with a profound excess of meaning. We, humans, are a problem to ourselves. The things we make—especially works of art, including poems—help us navigate this problem that we are. They help us to understand ourselves and our world, and they do so not merely by pronouncing answers or promoting ideologies (though they *can* do that, and they are worth interrogating when they do), but by various and unpredictable strategies of intellectual and affective involvement. The common materials they use to do this are the dimensions of language that are resistant, slippery, beautiful, playful, song-like, strange, and imaginative, which sometimes call attention to the fact that they do not "mean" in any straightforward way. Isaiah 24, for example, is one of the poems of the Bible that exploits most fully the euphonic dimensions of language. Here is one line (I include a nontechnical transliteration so that it can be "heard" by readers who do not know Hebrew. Note that I use a dash to indicate where two English words are translating one Hebrew word):

> 'avelah navelah ha'arets
> 'umlelah navelah tevel
> 'umlalu merom 'am-ha'arets

> It-mourns, withered (is) the-earth.
> It-languishes, withered (is) the-world.
> They-languish, exalted (are) the-people-of-the-land. (Isaiah 24:4)

These lines are clearly artful—the use of internal rhyme and word-play mark the lines and bind them together, and the poet uses related words that come from different Hebrew root forms to create a correspondence between what the earth does (mourns, for example), and what happens to them (it is withered, though we do not yet know by what). The lines also evince some ambiguity—the syntax of the final line of the triplet can be read in different ways: Are we meant to understand that it is the exalted people who now languish, or that in their languishing is some kind of devastating exaltation? Either way, the contrast seems ironic. The lines set us up to anticipate an explanation for this terrible situation, and the poet indeed gives one (Isaiah 24:5–6), but that doesn't seem to be the sole point, as the poem immediately turns back to develop further some of the imagery and sonic devices in the lines that follow. They establish a curious sense of alternation between silence and sound: they emphasize devastation and silence ("stilled is the merriment of timbrels," v. 8), but then evoke a loud cry, presumably a cry of anguish (v. 11), and then singing and rejoicing (v. 14). In the same breath, the speaker hears singing ("glory to the righteous!" v. 16) and then immediately breaks into an exclamation of distress:

> razi-li razi-li 'oy-li

> I waste, I waste, Woe is me! (Isaiah 24:16)

The "meaning" of *razi-li* is not certain because the word *raz* occurs only here. From an aesthetic perspective, the uncertainty is not a total hindrance because the poem is already using soundplay to push toward the edges of meaning. The word that follows it, *'oy*, I have translated "woe," but it is an outcry, an exclamation, like "ah," or "oh," or simply "oy." The experience of the poem makes the reader reckon with non-semantic dimensions of language: words that are cries and exclamations, expressions of emotions as much or more than carriers of content. How do such expressions verge on silence? When are they the only appropriate speech? When does language break down? When human cultures have failed, as the poet contends they have ("they broke the ancient covenant," v. 5), what can it mean to speak the language of that culture? When our speech presses toward non-meaning, why do we continue to speak, and how can we continue to listen? The poem is not simply promoting a forceful rhetoric in an oracle meant to drive people to faithfulness (though it could be instrumentalized in that way). The poem is also creating an experience of encounter that foregrounds the limits of language and the dissolution of sense. It might press us to wonder about the devastating beauty of a cry that comes from pain and becomes a pretext and a subject for a work of art. It might even help us ask ourselves about the limits of our ability to communicate, and the extravagant, embodied excesses of meaning we can experience when we find and cross those limits. In the shift to recognizing the poem as an encounter, it is useful to move away from the question, "What does it mean?" Instead we might ask: "Why does the poem look or sound the way it does? What are the problems that occupy it? What experience does it offer? What kinds of work does it accomplish?"

This book is an invitation to see the ancient Hebrew poetry collected in the Bible as part of a much broader human tradition of making art with words. I have kept technical jargon and footnotes to a minimum, and I have tried to use language accessible to students, general readers, and academics across other disciplines. One reason for this is that my approach assumes continuity between poems in the Bible and other traditions and literatures. Because I am a native English speaker, a North American, and an academic, much of my language reflects the traditions of English poetry and the vocabulary that has developed in Anglo-American universities for talking about poetry. And there is insight to be gained here: a central conviction of this book is that there is much in common between biblical poems and the poems you might encounter in an anthology of English language poetry, in spoken-word performances, or in song lyrics. These are all art made of words. But there are weaknesses to this approach, which I will touch on from time to time. One way this shows up is in our general ignorance about how the poetry of the Bible was composed, performed, heard, and remembered in the ancient world. I have tried to talk now and again about the "audience" of the poem (instead of the "reader") to gesture to the possibility of poetry's oral/aural and public dimensions. At the same time, the way many people today encounter the texts is through practices of private reading—and this too is a valid, rich way to encounter a poem. My social location is Western. But the texts are ancient, from southwest Asia, and many of them have some origin in the worship of the West Semitic deity Yahweh (hereafter "Yhwh," or "The Lord" in deference to the religious tradition of reverence for the divine name). The texts do not fundamentally belong to contemporary readers; having left the minds, mouths, and pens of the ancient poets, they become ours only for a time. We read them, speak them, inhabit them, and then they pass beyond us. We must therefore be aware of the provisional nature of our work, attending to the features and dynamics of biblical poems as we encounter them, describing as best we can their structures and style, aided by our own cultural and scholarly traditions.

To do so is to involve oneself in the messy tasks of reading, which implicate us in profound ways. Susan Sontag's essay "Against Interpretation" ends with a famous call for a new way of approaching art: "In place of a hermeneutics we need an erotics of art," in which the work of criticism entails "a really accurate, sharp, loving description of the appearance of a work of art."[4] Like Noë, Sontag's concern is that reducing a work of art to its "explanation" has a deflating, reductive effect. I think this is why she warns against "interpretation" and "hermeneutics." By imagining that the encounter with the text is an "erotic" one, Sontag compels us to think about how our own bodies are involved in and necessary to our aesthetic practices. On this view, we approach art with all the emotional, spiritual, physical complexity of our embodied human lives. This is true for worshippers who sing or pray the psalms and feel them in their lungs and throats and mouths, vibrating with the voices of their communities; it is true for readers who are drawn into the emotional drama and psychological depth of Job's debate with his friends; it is true for lovers who find themselves swept into the expansive, congenial world of the Song of Songs with its romantic saturation and lilting, springtime cadences; it is equally true for audiences who are compelled to disgust or shame or anger by some of the terrifying imagery of the prophets. These are bodily experiences. The poems ask us to feel with them. Sontag writes, "What is important now is to recover our senses. We must learn to *see* more, to *hear* more, to *feel* more."[5]

We might extend this insight further to think about the encounter with the poem as a place of encountering the other, where we come to hear, speak, feel, and think with our ancient forebears—people so different from ourselves—about the meaning of human life, the nature of the world, and the life of faith. All our evidence suggests that the ancient poets took their craft quite seriously. (It is helpful to remember that for the ancients, poetry was one place where the voice of God can be heard.) But there is equally evidence of joy and even playfulness among biblical poems. We might take these two things together as a signal about how to approach the texts—with both utter seriousness and the open mind of delight. Part of the serious work of reading poems from a recognized canon is to interrogate the nature of canon itself—to wonder why some texts are included (and not others), to wonder why some voices are included (and not others), and to resist some voices when it is morally urgent to do so. At the same time, one reason to keep reading poems is exactly because they do not easily conform to our current needs. To wrestle with a text, even a troublesome one, can give us pleasure, a kind of pleasure that is not exhausted by one reader, or one reading, or one meaning. The pleasure of a poem's language is the pleasure of all language—it makes possible the intimate experience of the world beyond ourselves. And yet, the satisfaction a poem gives is not in the fact that it is fully knowable or fully conforms to our intentions or ideas or political agendas. (How could it? Even poems we ourselves write do not do that, as poets sometimes recognize, to their amusement or chagrin.) Rather, part of the poem's appeal is in the way it persists in eluding us. Poetic language heightens the slippery dimensions of communication—it plays there, exploring the possibilities that lie at the far edge of meaning. Part of the delight of the poem is in our confrontation with something inexhaustible. We can return to the poem, again and again, and find new things there.

In what follows, I set out to describe some of the levels at which these poems operate. I begin with chapters devoted to the immediate material qualities of the biblical poems: Chapter 1 considers the "voices" that seem to speak with, to, or for us. What kinds of voices do we encounter here, and how do they speak? I will argue that voicing is a prominent dimension of biblical poems (as it is in other bodies of poetry), though it has generally not been foregrounded in other treatments of biblical poetry. Foregrounding voice is a unique contribution of this book. Chapter 2 explores how the poems are verbal arts organized more or less tightly into brief units of thought and sound, that is, in "lines." Lines are the most often discussed dimension of biblical poetry, and the tendency of biblical poets to group them through the iterative technique of parallelism has been a bit of a scholarly obsession. In this chapter, instead of tracking parallelism as a way of accounting for (or proving the existence of) biblical poetry, I ask instead: How do these techniques of lineation contribute to the aesthetic shape of texts, and how are they themselves ways of exploring meaning?

In chapter 3, I take a broader view of the corpus of biblical poetry, considering how individual poems participate in larger literary patterns, or "forms." I use the general term "form" differently from many biblical scholars, where the term has been captive to a school of thought that sees poems as windows into their social and ritual historical contexts. I am not using the term in this way. However, I retain the use the term "form" for several reasons: First, because it is the language of the broader literary disciplines and has the advantage of being both nontechnical and widely recognizable. Second, I find the term indispensable for talking about the way artworks participate in traditional patterns (genres) and at the same time are themselves indissolubly their material organization and their content. The word "structure," for example, cannot bear that weight. As I argue, biblical poetry is a fairly traditional body of verse, bound by many conventions. These traditions and conventions both constrain and liberate the creativity of the poems, which can use forms to profound and even surprising effect.

Chapter 4 considers a central tool of poets—the making of "figures." There are many treatments of metaphor in literary studies and in biblical studies more broadly. My approach stresses not the cognitive dimensions of metaphor, but the freedom of the poet in working within what is nevertheless a fairly conservative tradition. My framework is informed by some literary theorists who have emphasized the decided openness and indeterminacy of texts. Here, I begin to consider how the poet must rely on the audience to complete images and comparisons that are open or implicit, pressing beyond the bounds of the poem itself. The careful reader will note that I do not assume that the text is closed or that its meaning is fixed in a neat literary world. Instead, this chapter charts some of the ways that the text is always embroiled in the social and cultural dimensions of the world it emerges from, and it relies on (and is always also embroiled in) the social and cultural worlds of its interpreters. To engage in a close reading of the text is not therefore politically neutral, it is charged with potential: it is where the poem *happens*.

Finally, in chapter 5, I expand my consideration to ask how "contexts" shape poems—both the past contexts from which they emerge and the future contexts in which they are read and realized. Here is where my analysis embraces most fully the ways that poems are complexly historically determined and also stubbornly persistent. The long history of biblical interpretation (its "afterlives" or its "reception history") is not merely a record of that complexity, it is also an avenue for testing what troubles or compels us about texts and for revealing what remains outside of our grasp. Each chapter foregrounds biblical poems, showing by way of illustration a few of the possibilities of poetic technique. The discussions are by no means exhaustive. Each chapter ends with a reading of a psalm that offers an acute example of the dimension under discussion. I have chosen to do this because it is one implicit argument of this book that anything we learn from or about art must have the work of art at its center. It is my attempt to answer Sontag's call for "a really accurate, sharp, loving description of the appearance of a work of art."

As I hope will become clear over the course of the book, I do not believe there is a single theory that accounts for the diversity of poems we encounter in the Bible. And it is not clear that the ancient Israelites and Judahites who wrote, edited, and collected the poetry of the Bible had a neatly worked out theory about what poetry is either. If they did, we have no extant evidence for it. But they did preserve a wide variety of texts composed largely in parallelistic lines that are sometimes richly evocative, occasionally quite provocative, often composed with rhythmic, allusive, oversaturated language. Just as there are many different reasons that people write poems today—as formal exercises, as expressions of individual experience, as communal rituals, as a way of channeling the divine, as political statements, as a form of prayer—there are many different ways to account for the appearances of the various poems in the Bible. As you will notice in the chapter titles, I assume that all the dimensions discussed can be usefully talked about in the plural: "voices," instead of "voice," for example. While all biblical poems use "voices" (see chapter 1), they do not all assume a consistent tenor or position or articulation or audience. These poems are not all alike, and we should not assume that the ancient poets or their audiences assumed they were all alike. As much is anticipated in Ezekiel's concern over the perception of his vocation: "Ah, my Lord Yhwh, they are saying of me 'is he not a maker of metaphors?'" (Ezekiel 20:49 [Heb. 21:5]; see also 33:32). His specific phrase, *memashel meshalim*, which I translate "maker of metaphors," is mellifluous and expressive. It suggests one who creates verbal arts. My point here is this: Ezekiel thinks about his poetry in one way (as not "merely" poetry, but poetry that requires a response); his audience thinks about his poetry in quite another way (as "merely" poetry, perhaps as a frivolity). It seems to me that what is at stake is not whether Ezekiel has created art, but how that art is received, considered, and valued. Ezekiel's chagrin points to a specific truth: there is more than one way to interpret a poem, and more than one context in which poems make sense. This pluripotentiality of biblical poems is one of their common features, one that has made them open to successive generations of new readers.

I end here with a note of encouragement for reluctant readers. Many people find poetry to be a source of frustration, an arduous task rather than an opportunity for expansiveness and insight. At the first lines of a poem, readers may throw up their hands: "What does it mean?" "I don't get it!" The feeling is perhaps something like standing, lost, in a hedge maze, where tall boxwoods present a seemingly impenetrable wall—only this wall is made of words. If the point of reading a poem is to get to the center, its "meaning," then the poet has given us a difficult, obstructed path. But the poem is not a maze for which we need a map or a room for which we have lost the key.[6] It might be helpful to use a different metaphor: What if the poem is more like a labyrinth, which the reader is invited to walk? Reading a poem has in common with the labyrinth a certain directed aimlessness. In a labyrinth, there are no dead ends. One walks in a deliberate path. But it is at the same time a nondirectional walking, one that involves winding back, revisiting a previous part of the circle. There are no wrong turns. Reading a poem involves a process of revision in which new lines draw us back to a reconsideration of previous ones. The direction of the poem is forward, as the direction of the labyrinth is certain. But one does not walk with a particular destination in mind—neither the labyrinth nor the poem has a "goal," a standard of success measured by achieving the "correct" meaning. Rather, the poem presents questions for us: Will you give your time and attention? How will you see the world when you turn this corner? What is familiar, and what surprises? And perhaps, when you arrive at the end, what new vantage do you have? This book will offer a guide to help readers gain confidence as they encounter biblical poems. But there is no replacement for simply reading. Like a labyrinth, a poem has no shortcut. It asks its audience to invest time, energy, care, and above all, attention. As we do so, we access a sacred opportunity to become "collaborators," to use Noë's term, in the experience and knowledge of the poem.

1

Voices

TO READ BIBLICAL POEMS IS to encounter voices. These voices come to us over millennia, from people distant in language, culture, and time. Yet over the centuries, readers of these poems have often remarked that these voices feel familiar, even personal. How do biblical poems accomplish this sense of human connection?

It is a distinctive quality of biblical poems that they appear to be spoken *by* someone. Consider the opening lines of the great love poem of the Bible, the Song of Songs:

> Let him kiss me with the kisses of his mouth,
> for your love is better than wine! (Song 1:2)

A woman's voice commands our attention. The first word, "let him kiss me" foregrounds erotic desire unapologetically as the subject of the text. Notice how the mouth, lovemaking, and wine create a delicious and heady atmosphere charged with sensuality. This voice is vibrant and perhaps audacious. Though her audience in the first line is not yet identified, she appears to be in dialogue from the outset, and we will soon encounter the address and response of the daughters of Jerusalem. In the second line, however, she shifts from speaking about her lover to addressing him directly: "*your* love is better than wine." In poetry, "voice takes place not merely as a presence but as the condition under which that person appears." An encounter with the other happens through voice, made possible by language and by our willingness to listen: "The realization

An Invitation to Biblical Poetry. Elaine T. James, Oxford University Press. © Oxford University Press 2022.
DOI: 10.1093/oso/9780190664923.003.0002

of expression depends on the *bind*, the implicit tie of intelligibility between speaker and listener that links their efforts."[1]

In the Song of Songs, the entire poem is an exchange of direct discourse: first-person "I" speech predominates, and much of it is directed to a beloved other, to "you."[2] The lovers engage by speaking and by listening to one another. The "I" voice—or the "we" voice in communally voiced texts—can give the impression of being deeply personal. Readers identify with the voices of these poems as they read them, momentarily taking on their perspectives and dispositions. This is different from saying that poems with an "I" offer a straightforward disclosure of a unique, subjective individual who wrote the poem. In biblical poetry, the idiosyncratic dimensions of individual identity tend to be suppressed in favor of a more open, paradigmatic "I"—while the "I" can disclose a character, it can equally belong to anyone who picks up the text.[3]

Throughout the Song, the woman continues to elaborate her desire in intimate and charged acclamations:

> Sustain me with raisins,
> refresh me with apples,
> for I am sick with love.
> His right hand was under my head
> and his left hand embraced me. (Song 2:5–6)

Here, the commands "sustain" and "refresh" are plural forms—to what people is she speaking? It might include her friends; it implicitly includes us, the readers. To her speeches the lover responds, describing his desire in terms of her beauty:

> How beautiful you are, my love,
> how very beautiful.
> Your eyes are doves behind your veil. (Song 4:1)

The poem unfolds through this exchange of dialogue, a give-and-take of lovers' speeches that expands occasionally outward, inviting other voices. There is no story here, no third-person narration setting the scene, giving us backstory, or even telling us what happens. Instead, the voices of these lovers conjure an atmosphere in which they—and we readers—revel in a rich aesthetic of the body and of language. This lack of story is characteristic of Hebrew poems. Unlike a play, in which the dialogue is in service to a plot, here there is no plot. The dialogue itself is what happens. The poems lead us into a sense of the interior world of the speakers, who are consumed with the emotions of love. The poems are their speech.

EMOTION AND THE BODY

To take a grimmer example, early in the book of Genesis, we encounter a brief poem in the voice of Lamech:

> Adah and Zillah, hear my voice!
> O wives of Lamech, give ear to my word.
> For a man I have killed for my bruise,
> and a boy for my wound.
> Surely Cain was avenged sevenfold,
> but Lamech seventy-sevenfold. (Genesis 4:23–24)

Again, this is first-person speech. The "I" of the poem offers a window into the character's subjectivity by projecting an interior landscape.

The narrative that surrounds, in contrast, is third-person discourse. Its narrator recounts events about people that occur in another place and time:

> Lamech took two wives; the name of the one was Adah, and
> the name of the second was Zillah. Adah bore Jabal; he was
> the ancestor of those who live in tents and have livestock.
> The name of his brother was Jubal; he was the ancestor of all

those who play the lyre and the pipe. And Zillah: she bore
Tubal-cain, forger of all implements of bronze and iron. The
sister of Tubal-cain was Naamah. (Genesis 4:19–22)

The poetic lines lack that narrative quality. They do not tell a story,
and the subject is not given by a narrator. Instead, they give voice to a
character. The poem even calls attention to this voiced-ness: "Adah
and Zillah, *hear my voice.*" Within biblical narrative, poems are now
and again inset in this way: they change the pace and tone of the
narrative, integrating what are likely older, traditional poems, into
the stories. (This is the case, for example, with Moses' and Miriam's
songs in Exodus 15; with Deborah's song in Judges 5; and Hannah's
in 1 Samuel 2). Note how spare the narrative is: we are given no
details at all about the conflicts around which the poem centers
or any character's experiences or feelings. The poem, however,
fairly explodes with Lamech's sense of indignation and gestures to
a character who is both beset by enemies and bent on executing
justice for himself. The rising intensity of the lines (from "man" to
"boy," from "sevenfold" to "seventy-sevenfold") magnifies his sense
of injustice and, perhaps, our sense of his unchecked cruelty. One
thing that poems set into the narrative do is offer expansions of
psychological and emotional experience and character that we do
not otherwise get in biblical narrative.[4]

The voice implies the body. To assert one's voice is to project
from the body, and to listen to another's voice is an act of reception. In the Song of Songs, this assertion and reception of bodily
selves is a matter of reciprocal desire. In Lamech's poem, too, the
voice is a projection of embodiment. It is projected through the
verbal summoning of his audience at the beginning of each of
the first two lines, each of which ends with a marked emphasis on
voice and speech:

Adah and Zillah, hear my voice!
O wives of Lamech, give ear to my word. (Genesis 4:23)

"My voice" and "my word" highlight the personal dimension of his speech. This is developed through the evocation of his own body in the second couplet, each line of which ends with a reference to his woundedness at the hand of some anonymous assailant: "for my bruise," "for my wound." The last two couplets offer a building comparison that hinges on the single verb, "was avenged" (*yuqqam*). The voice of the poem is instigated on behalf of the body of the speaker, which becomes the central focus of the poem: four lines in a row end with the first-person suffix -*i* "my". We, with Lamech's wives, are asked to consider the "I" of Lamech's embodied experience. The voice is the intermediary between self and other, between language and the body.[5]

There are many questions we cannot answer about this short poem. Noting that it is framed as a voice, speaking *about* voice, helps us key into some of its dynamics. We do not know why Lamech directs his speech toward his wives, Adah and Zillah, whom he expressly names (directing a speech toward a named woman is uncommon in biblical poetry). We do not know why Lamech refers to himself in the third person (again, uncommon in biblical poetry). But these three names provide a frame of knowability for the center lines of the poem, which by contrast evoke nameless violence: "a man" and "a boy" are the center of the poem, whom he boasts about avenging, while not specifying who they are. We might note the strangeness and distastefulness of these lines, but the text neither enshrines nor explicitly critiques Lamech and leaves such judgments to the reader, who, in light of the narrative context, might understand them to signal the rising tide of human violence that begins with Cain and results in flood. Nevertheless, we can see how the poem uses these strategies of voice to effect an experience. They foreground the personal, bodily experience of the speaker while bolstering his sense of pervasive, anonymous violence that must be contained and controlled. Part of that containment is achieved by the vengeance he boasts of, but its containment is further enacted through the poem's assertion of voice.

In the book of Exodus we encounter quite a different voice: the prophetic voice of Miriam. According to the narrative setting, Miriam's liturgical leadership offers a ritual of victory: "Miriam the prophet, sister of Aaron, took a tambourine in her hand, and all the women went out after her with tambourines and dancing. And Miriam sang to them" (Exodus 15:20). The poem (or what remains of it) is just one couplet:

> Sing to Yhwh for he has surely triumphed:
> Horse and rider he has hurled into the sea. (Exodus 15:21)

The lines, though brief, show us several things. The opening word "sing" tells us something about ancient poetry, namely its deep connection to both performance and to music. While culturally the Western literary tradition has tended to characterize poetry as a private, quiet art, the performative dimension is often on display in biblical texts. This suggests that the texts were not only intended for personal consumption but might have been more like scripts that could be re-performed for an audience. The lack of widespread literacy in the ancient world makes this oral/aural dimension all the more salient. If you cannot read, your experience of poetry will be hearing and remembering, reciting or singing. Singing especially shifts the priority of the poem away from the semantic content of the words themselves (which become less distinct in vocal performance) while adding a musical dimension that we cannot recreate (but perhaps we can imagine). We would expect this to contribute to a surplus of meaning not accessible in contemporary practices of private reading—one of the limits I alluded to in the introduction. The performative dimension is not limited to the ancient context, either. In the contemporary world, both the lyricism of popular music and the widespread appeal of spoken word poetry suggest that communal staging of poetry is alive and well. This particular text from Exodus has a place in contemporary Jewish and Christian liturgies, where its performance continues to be key. Communities, ancient and modern, perform their poems in both speech and song.

Here again, the poem serves as a site of emotional self-presentation: It memorializes a great event with the buoyancy and exhilaration of praise. It invites us to *feel* something, to feel it with Miriam and the Israelites at the edge of the sea, and to feel it with the others who have read, recited, and sung these words over the centuries. These lines do not offer the same sense of individual emotion that we see in the Song and in Lamech's poem. Instead, it is staged as a command to a group of people to a shared embodied experience: "Sing!" The song's ebullience is amplified by the surrounding narrative details of dancing and making music with tambourines. We also detect a kind of self-assertion in the prophet Miriam's voice, who speaks with commanding authority over a group of people. Such acts have gendered dimensions. Women's speech is often censored or overwritten in biblical texts—and, indeed, in other ancient and contemporary contexts, as well.[6] It may be the case that the more elaborate poem of Exodus 15 signals a reappropriation of Miriam's song under male auspices. While this poem preserves a moment of feminine self-assertion without qualifying or commenting on it, a story in the book of Numbers will record the bodily punishment of Miriam for her exercise of prophetic speech.[7] As projections of the body, we expect voices to bear the marks of gendered bodily experience (for further discussion, see "Gender and Voice" later in this chapter).

Already with these three short texts we begin to get a sense of the range of voice and emotion one can encounter in biblical poems. There is no emotion the biblical poets shied away from. The complexity and diversity of human affective experience, in all its beauty and all its ugliness, is on display. We encounter explorations of faithfulness and joy along with base lust for violence and vengeance; soaring hope as well as utter despondency; laughter and joy as well as shame and fear. These ancient voices echo and valorize the full range of human experience. When characters speak in biblical narrative, they often do so in poetry, expanding the emotional and descriptive qualities of the text. The otherwise hidden dimensions of human psychology are the province of these poems. This is not to make a universal claim about what *all* poetry does or can do (though certainly some have made exactly this claim about poetry in general, that its domain is human emotion).[8] But it is certainly the case for these ancient poems. While the writers of biblical narrative tended to suppress or conceal the dimensions of desire, motivation, turbulent process of thought, and the inner workings of human emotion, the writers of biblical poetry revel in it.[9]

ASCRIPTION AND AUTHORSHIP

Now, a caveat: I have been speaking of Lamech and Miriam as characters. I do so not to suggest they are necessarily fictional but to remind the reader of an obvious but important point: because they are poems, they are composed by poets. Most poems are not spontaneous autobiographical outpourings, but are products of reflection, craft, and technique. The voice that the poem speaks with is not necessarily identical to the voice of the poet, who is of course free to take up and use personae other than their own. The dramatic poetry of Robert Browning (e.g., his famous poem, "My Last Duchess") is one example. A modern example: American poet Lucille Clifton wrote many poems from the perspective and voice of historical and literary characters. Clifton's poems showcase how voice can be a technique to explore a psyche and story beyond one's experience. In "brothers," Clifton's series of eight poems that enact a conversation between Lucifer and God, we hear only Lucifer's voice. This is simply to note that there is not a confusion between the poet and the voice of the poem. We do not mistake the persona of the poem (in this case Lucifer) for a historical person or for the author (in this case Lucille Clifton). Rather, the poem becomes a site of exploration that uses voice as a technique in service to its artistic vision. This modern example offers a parallel for thinking about the evocation of the voices of biblical characters. So, when I speak of the poem's "voice" I do not mean that we have access to the person and psychology of a historical Lamech or a historical Miriam. I mean that biblical poems are cast as speech, and as such, we encounter them as voices. Because the poet's voice may be different from the poem's voice, there is an inherent multiplicity of voices in any given text (and when we read and re-read them in our own voices, we add yet more layers of multiplicity).

This distinction is especially important because many (though not all) poems in the Bible are ascribed to particular people. Many of the psalms, for example, are associated with the name of David: *ledavid* "of David" is attached to the beginning of seventy-three psalms, some of which further relate the psalm to an event in the narrative of David's life.[10] Other psalms are associated with Asaph, with the "sons of Korah," and a few others with other figures. This reflects the well-known ancient practice of associating important texts with important people. While it is of course possible that some of the psalms do go back to a Davidic pen, as it were, it is not likely that all of them do. Rather, the scribes who curated these ancient texts created powerful associations by gathering texts together under the name of such an iconic figure in biblical tradition.[11]

The resonances of David's story, when they are filtered through the voice of this complex, ultimately tragic hero of the biblical tradition, amplify our reading of the psalms and enrich the traditions about David's character. For example, Psalm 51 includes a brief ascription relating the psalm to the moment in the narrative of David's life "when the prophet Nathan came to him, after he had gone into Bathsheba," a story told in 2 Samuel 12. The text of the poem itself does not point definitively to David—its language speaks in general terms about seeking mercy and purification from sin. But readers (ancient and modern) who are keyed into the narrative about David will fill in details, letting the narrative inform the poem. Lines like these assume fuller meaning when readers relate them to David's story of adultery and murderous desire:

> Create for me a clean heart, O God,
> a new and right spirit within me. (Psalm 51:10)

The psalm also amplifies the character of David as a pious and penitential figure (not a triumphant king), which is a consistent emphasis in the ascriptions of many psalms relating to David.[12] This enriches the story of his character, who in the narrative of 2 Samuel 12 says in response to Nathan only "I have sinned against the Lord"—not exactly an extravagant or obviously devout show of penitence.

But perhaps more importantly, through these ascriptions David becomes a model for later people who read or pray them and who identify with him, especially during times of crisis or anguish. It is a remarkable quality of the first-person voice of poetry that when readers take up the poem, they assume the voice of the speaker. Their own "I" becomes the voice of the poem.[13] In this way, the poem is not merely the outpourings of an Iron Age king or an ancient poet; rather it is the voice of our own despair. The poem's utterance of the "I" compels us to articulate ourselves in a particular way—as people in need of forgiveness, for example. While the speaker says, "I know my transgressions, / and my sin is ever before me" (Psalm 51:3), the poem never specifies the "transgressions," either David's or our own. The poem remains radically open to the being over-voiced and re-appropriated in new contexts. Every reader who encounters this ancient text is thus positioned to ask questions about their own interiority, a process that requires a kind of reflective distance or even alienation from the experience of the self in the present moment.[14] Questions that arise from this distance in Psalm 51 might include the following: What are my transgressions? What have I done that might be "evil in your (God's) sight"? What wisdom do I need to be taught? How can I receive the gift of a "clean heart"? Psalm 51's voice is a voice of confession, but many psalms—even those that emphasize dejection—tend to treat misery as the result of enemies or circumstances, and position God as the divine deliverer, as in Psalm 22: "I am a worm and not human, / scorned by mortals, despised by people . . . You drew me from the womb, / entrusted me to my mother's breasts" (Psalm 22:6, 9). To utter such words reorients the self both to the experience of trouble and to the deity. It is part of the magic of such poems that when we read them, their voices become our own.

MULTIPLICITY AND DIALOGUE

Even within the same poem, we often see variations in the texture of voices.[15] Some of this variability in voicing appears to be linked to poetry's performative dimensions. Many psalms, for example, seem to have been composed for and performed in public liturgies and rituals, and they reflect those contexts by including refrains and antiphonal responses between congregation and leader:

> Give thanks to the Lord, for he is good;
> His steadfast love is eternal!
> Let Israel say,
> "His steadfast love is eternal!"
> Let the house of Aaron say,
> "His steadfast love is eternal!" (Psalm 118:1–3)

This antiphonal dimension is sometimes phrased in a question-answer format, such as in Psalm 24, where nearly the whole psalm is shaped by this call-and-response dimension, which makes it easy to imagine a congregation assembled in public worship reciting a prayer in a ritual context:

> Who may ascend the hill of Yhwh?
> And who may stand in his holy place?

The clean of hands and pure of heart,
who has not lifted up his soul to what is false,
and has not sworn deceitfully . . .

Who is this King of glory?
Yhwh of hosts:
He is the king of glory. (Psalm 24:3–4, 10)

The call-and-response of hymns like this one reveal how the voices of biblical poems are not just the voices of individuals in prayerful self-reflection (though such voices are robustly present). Psalms can also embed multiple voices. In Psalm 10, to take another example, part of the speaker's meditation is on the fickle and confident words of the enemies, which are quoted within the psalm: " 'There is no God' "; "They think in their heart, 'God has forgotten, / he has hidden his face, he will never see it' " (Psalm 10:4, 11). These quoted voices serve as a foil for the speaker's own conviction that God will indeed "see" and will work justice for the oppressed:

Rise up, Yhwh, lift up your hand!
Do not forget the oppressed.
Why does the wicked person renounce God,
and say in his heart, "You will not investigate"?
Surely you see trouble and vexation;
you take note, in order to take action.
The helpless commit themselves to you;
you have been the helper of the orphan. (Psalm 10:12–14)

Here, the primary voice evokes the counter-voice of the enemy in order to critique its claim to philosophical superiority. The voice of the enemy denies God and simultaneously addresses God with its denial. It stands in tension with the primary voice's affirmation of God's justice. The intentional use of contrasting voices bolsters the sense that divine care for the marginalized might overcome even the most recalcitrant and exploitative forces. These examples showcase the multiplicity of voices one might expect to encounter, even within a single poem.

At times, this multiplicity of voices is stretched even further. In the poetry of Job, the tension between voices takes on a much more pronounced and contentious quality. Like the Song of Songs, the great part of the book of Job (3:1–42:6) is cast as a dialogue between characters in a dramatic encounter. Job's voice opens the dialogue with a poem that calls for the annihilation of his day of birth, beckoning the deep darkness of nonbeing, calling for the only peace he can imagine in his state of suffering—the peace of the grave (Job 3:3–26). It is a harrowing poem, in which the imagery repeatedly evokes the extinguishing of light. His three friends, Eliphaz, Bildad, and Zophar, offer responses to Job and Job responds to each of them in turn. A fourth character, Elihu, also speaks to Job later in the book, to which Job never responds. Each character speaks with a fairly unique voice. Eliphaz speaks with the voice of an elderly visionary; Elihu's is the voice of youthful confidence. Perhaps the most striking is the virulent Zophar, who fairly explodes with indignation over what he perceives to be Job's inability to understand the most basic dimensions of wisdom:

> Do you not know this from of old,
> when mortals were placed on earth,
> . that the rejoicing of the wicked is short-lived,
> and the joy of the godless is momentary? (Job 20:4–5)

The diction and imagery of the poem builds progressively along with Zophar's outrage. The wicked will perish like their own dung (v. 7); they grotesquely hold wickedness under their tongues until they are forced to vomit it up again (vv. 13–15); their fate is to be thrust through by a sword that will come out the other side, covered in bile (v. 25). With this appalling language Zophar's poem

reads like a rant. The poet of this great work has created persuasive, compelling voices that are radically distinct—and has managed to efface his own voice so effectively that it is not always
clear whose perspective is favored. The dialogue of the book of
Job creates an irreconcilable tension between these voices.[16] Even
the voice of God, speaking from the whirlwind at the end of the
book (Job 38–41), enters the fray of this densely philosophical
debate:

> Is it through your understanding the hawk soars,
> spreads his wings to the south? (Job 39:26)
>
> Gird up your loins like a man!
> I will ask you, and you will enlighten me.
> Would you even violate my justice,
> condemning me to justify yourself?
> Have you an arm like God?
> And with a voice like his can you thunder? (Job 40:7–9)

These selections from the Yhwh poems gives a small sample of
how the Joban poet imagines the divine voice. It is a voice of
power and authority, and Job's response to it is one of cowed
submission: "Look, I am small. / What can I answer you?" (Job
40:4). And yet, if this were the only voice the poet thought
worthwhile, why develop thirty-five chapters of some of the
most intriguingly voiced, artfully wrought poetry in the Bible?
The poet appears to be playing with the technique of voice. The
reader's experience must shift among these various contrasting
points of view, with some necessary mix of investment, consideration, and judgment. The process of reading enacts the
testing of the philosophical complexity of wisdom, suffering,
and submission, and readers are positioned through the process to try, adopt, or reject different voices—and perhaps
thereby to find their own.

PROPHETIC VOICING

The prophetic books use voicing in intriguing and multiple ways. Instead of speaking *to* God (as the psalms overwhelmingly do) or as characters *to* other characters (as both the Song of Songs and the book of Job do), prophetic poetry primarily speaks to an audience *as* or *on behalf of God*. It is God's voice. Some biblical traditions figure the divine voice as non-linguistic: it is a sound like thunder—powerful, magnificent, even terrifying in its dimensions.[17] But its linguistic expression, almost without exception, takes the form of poetry. As Robert Alter writes:

> Since poetry is our best human model of intricately rich communication, not only solemn, weighty, and forceful but also densely woven with complex internal connections, meanings, and implications, it makes sense that divine speech should be represented as poetry.[18]

The poetry of Amos offers a good and very famous example of this kind of prophetic voicing:

> I hate, I despise your festivals,
> and I am not appeased by your solemn assemblies.
> If you offer me your burnt offerings
> and grain offerings, I will not accept them . . .
> But let justice roll down like waters,
> and righteousness like a never-failing stream. (Amos 5:21–24,
> excerpts)

The speaking voice is God's: ("you offer me your burnt offerings"), and the rhetoric is fittingly powerful ("I hate, I despise"). The poem moves inexorably forward on the rising scale of its imagery, which bursts forth like water released from a dam. The voice and imagery of the poem work together to create the

forceful moral condemnation and to make compelling the demand for change.

This is speech oriented toward an audience, which you can see
here in the command "seek me":

> For thus says Yhwh to the house of Israel:
> Seek me and live. (Amos 5:4)

There is the expectation that an audience is listening and, as a result of
the poem, might respond. Many of the prophetic poems are like this.
God urges the people to act or to change their behavior. But inter-
leaved within the divine voice is the prophet's voice. They are inextricable in many poems, the prophet's voice and the divine voice, and
so the poems already contain a clear sense that the human mediation
of the divine message is necessary, even desirable. This interleaving is
visible in Amos 5, where the poem shifts almost immediately from
"Seek me" to speaking about God in the third person: "Seek Yhwh
and live, / lest he rush like fire the house of Joseph" (Amos 5:6). This
is a slippery conflation, where the voice moves from God's voice, to
the prophet's, and back again. It allows the poet to invite the audience
to admire the power and grandeur of God while also speaking with
the conviction of the deity's sense of justice:

> The maker of Pleiades and Orion,
> who turns to morning the deepest darkness
> and darkens day into night,
> who summons the waters of the sea,
> and pours them out on the face of the earth:
> Yhwh is his name . . .
>
> For I know the profusion of your transgressions,
> and the multitude of your sins—
> who afflict the righteous, who take a bribe,
> and the needy in the gate they push aside. (Amos 5:8, 12)

The voicing of the prophetic texts, in other words, is highly dramatic in that it implies an audience and a shape-shifting speaker, who is at once a preacher, a performer, and an oracle delivering a message from God.

This modulation between the voice of God and the prophet is sometimes so fine that it is nearly impossible to discern with certainty who is speaking. In some texts from Jeremiah, for example, the voice of the prophet mingles almost completely with the voice of the deity. In one of the "confessions" of Jeremiah, there is no clear delineation between the voice of God and the voice of the prophet:

> Because my poor people are crushed, I am crushed.
> I mourn, and dismay seizes me.
> Is there no balm in Gilead?
> Is there no healer there?
> Then why is the health of my poor people not restored?
> Oh that my head were water,
> and my eyes a well of tears,
> that I might weep day and night
> for the slain of my poor people. (Jeremiah 8:21–9:1)

The *HarperCollins Study Bible* offers a subheading, "The Prophet Mourns for the People" in order to clarify the murky voicing of verses 18–22. But the Hebrew text includes no such heading. Sometimes translators offer similar, more subtle clarifications, by adding quotation marks. (Again, there are none in the Hebrew texts.) It is just as compelling to hear this not as the prophet's voice, but as the voice of God. Earlier, in Jeremiah 8:19, Yhwh speaks: "Why have they provoked me to anger with their images, with their foreign idols?" And the weeping section concludes with the divine voice: "They go from evil to evil, and they do not know me, says Yhwh" (Jeremiah 9:3). The point here is that the prophetic poem blends the prophet's voice with the divine voice. This blending, according to the account of these poems, is not a neutral one—Jeremiah is overcome by the divine voice, such that he does not fully control his own. Rather, body and voice are subjected to the compulsion of God, which is an experience of agony for the prophet.[19] One has the sense that the deity's grief has fully become the prophet's. The pathos of the prophet—to feel as God feels—is part of the technical plea of the poem.[20] The reader is invited through the poem's voicing to experience the same commingled passion, painful as that may be. Inhabiting the otherness of the divine voice perhaps also accounts for some of the disjointed dimensions of prophetic voice—its "stammering" multiplicity, which can border on incoherence.[21]

Occasionally, voice is specifically thematized by a prophetic text. In the case of Isaiah 15–16, a poem about the nation of Moab, the poem calls attention to its use of voice. The poem's central trope is the weeping of cities:

> She cries out, Heshbon and Elealeh;
> their voice is heard as far as Jahaz. (Isaiah 15:4)

Two Moabite cities, Heshbon and Elealeh, are personified here. Their voice rises and echoes across the breadth of the country of Moab (they are feminized—"she" in Hebrew). This trope of cities as weeping women is well-known from ancient laments. Here, it becomes a central engine for the speaker, who elaborates a sense of pathos for Moab's destruction (or imminent destruction?) by reiterating the weeping of places across the initial four verses of the poem. The voice is imagined as though it is on a journey—having traversed the country "as far as Jahaz." This anticipates the journey of the refugees who are also on a journey—walking "as far as Zoar and Eglath-shelishiyah" (v. 5). In addition to the voicing of the lines, Dibon goes "to weep" (v. 2), Moab "wails" (v. 2), and Moab "cries out" (v. 4). At the same time, the poem is densely saturated with Moabite place-names (Ar, Kir, Dibon, Nebo, Medeba, Heshbon, Elealeh, Jahaz, Zoar, Eglath-shelishiyah, Luhith, Nimrim, Eglaim, Beer-elim, Kir-hareseth, Sibmah). The effect is to bring insistently to mind the geography of destruction. The weeping of these personified cities merges with the voices of their inhabitants, who mourn. They all "wail" and "weep" (v. 3), and when the "I" voice of the poem emerges in verse 5, it too voices the same cry, even using one of the same verbs, *yiz'aq* "cry out" (also in v. 4):

> My heart for Moab cries out;
> her refugees flee to Zoar,
> to Eglath-shelishiyah. (Isaiah 15:5)

We do not (yet) know who the "I" is—it could be the prophet, it could be God. (Later in the poem it seems to be the divine voice, 15:9, 16:9.) But the voices of the destroyed cities are entwined with the voices of their fleeing inhabitants, which in turn affect the speaker's voice. To hear the voices of suffering bodies, this poem suggests, is to be infected bodily by their pain:

> Therefore my heart throbs for Moab like a harp,
> and my inner being for Kir-hareseth. (Isaiah 16:11)

This is remarkable because Moab is unexceptionally counted among Israel's enemies in biblical texts. In this poem, though, the weeping of the enemy engenders empathy. This is visible through the shift in voicing that takes place in Isaiah 16:3, where the lines now become commands that address an audience:

> Bring counsel.
> Work justice.
> Make your shade like night
> at the height of noon.
> Shelter the outcasts.
> Do not betray the refugees.
> Let the displaced of Moab
> settle among you.
> Be a refuge for them
> before the destroyer. (Isaiah 16:3–4)

The complex merging of voices in this poem (between the cities and their inhabitants; between God and the prophet) is one technique among others. In it, the voice is both emotionally vulnerable and an authority that makes demands on the hearer. Other techniques of the poem include wordplay, soundplay, and creative uses of imagery. As one of its principal techniques, this poem harnesses the voice's capacity to connect the bodies of different people in profoundly affecting ways. Hearing the voice of pain—even of one's enemy—positions the audience as the profoundly addressed, making possible the culminating call for the empathic extension of protection for the vulnerable.

GENDER AND VOICE

The voice, so closely linked to interiority, emotion, and the body, also connects the speaker through discourse to community. It is therefore a key place where identity is cultivated and performed, one dimension of which is gender. The voices of biblical poetry can be gender-neutral (the first-person "I" and "we" voices are particularly malleable and potentially inclusive) but often they are coded for gender. Gender is potentially marked in a variety of ways. Poems are often linked to a particular character (David, Hannah, Miriam, Lamech, Jonah, etc.), and in classical Hebrew, gender is marked grammatically. So, in the Song of Songs, for example, the reader can usually tell when the young woman is addressing the young man, and vice versa.[22] As such the speaking voice is often a gendered figure. Another way to think about gender is to consider how the content of a biblical poem may be characteristically or stereotypically gendered, as in the case of Psalm 131, which I will discuss. Studying voice in biblical poetry might therefore provide glimpses into ancient concepts of gender, which can be surprisingly complex and variable, despite their largely two-sex assumptions. A willingness to encounter those voices, and to take them into ourselves as readers, only adds to this complexity.[23]

The first point to note is that while most biblical poetry is identified with a male speaker (in the case of the Psalms, all the attributed poems are attributed to men), there are poems identified with female speakers. I will start with an exploration of a few of those texts. This exploration of voices as feminine figures is an important first step in thinking about gender in biblical poetry, given the overall androcentrism of the texts. These include the predominantly feminine voice of the Song of Songs, which speaks to a male lover and consistently evokes a world of other women (her mother, her friends):

> I would lead you, I would bring you
> into the house of my mother, she who taught me. (Song 8:2)

She also talks about herself, her voice confident and self-determined: "I am black and beautiful"; "My beloved is mine and I am his"; "Upon my bed at night, I sought him whom I love"; "I adjure you, O daughters of Jerusalem / do not stir up or awaken love until it is ready." Her speech is not contained or qualified by male speech. In fact, the opposite is the case: her voice dominates in the Song, and we occasionally hear the male voice through the quotational authority of hers: She says of him "My lover speaks and says to me . . . " (Song 2:10). A poem attributed to Ruth set into the narrative of the book of Ruth echoes the Song's emphasis on emotional attachment, as Ruth promises her devotion to her mother-in-law (Ruth 1:16–17). This shared theme of devoted love suggests that there may be some normative patterns of the gendered subject in biblical poetry (though, as we shall see momentarily, outpourings of love are not limited to women). That Ruth's devotion is directed to another woman challenges an idea of the thoroughgoing heteronormativity of women's voices in biblical texts. This challenge is issued through the figure of the feminine voice.

Thematically, we might expect women's poetry to be concerned with the domains of the household, the traditional locus

of women's labor in ancient Israel. But no poems survive from ancient Israel that center emphatically on childbearing, midwifery,
weaving, baking, household religion, or herbalism, though no
doubt such traditions also existed, at least orally.[24] There are a few
texts, not explicitly linked with women, whose content or tone
may be suggestive of women's culture—whether or not they may
have been written by women. A good example of this is Psalm 131,
which is short enough to cite in its entirety here:

> O Yhwh, my heart is not high;
> my eyes are not raised;
> I do not walk in greatness
> or in things too wonderful for me.
> Rather, I have calmed
> and quieted my soul.
> Like a sated child on his mother,
> my soul is like the sated child that is on me.
> Hope, O Israel, in Yhwh
> from now on and forever. (Psalm 131:1–3)

The line "my soul is like the sated child that is on me" positions
the speaker holding a child, traditionally a domain of wom-
en's work. Imagining the child resting "on" the speaker and also
sated ("weaned" is a possible reading) is an image that suggests
breastfeeding. The line has often been incorrectly translated as
something like: "my soul *within me* is like a weaned child." The
difference is subtle, but it has profound effect on our perception
of the poem's voicing (and on the anthropology of the text, and
our understanding of what and where the "soul" is, but that is another matter). A straightforward reading of this psalm could suggest a feminine speaker, though of course people of any gender can
hold sleepy children. The voice of the speaker in the poem figures
soothing maternal speech, replicating the primordial connection
between the crying baby and the calming mother. The redupli-
cated phrase "like a sated child" || "like the sated child" suggests

the mirroring of a connected parent-child relationship and enacts the comfort it describes. If the voicing is indeed feminine, the discourse of modesty might be a gendered dimension of the text, as it sometimes is in women's poetry (e.g., Anne Bradstreet's "The Author to Her Book").[25] Nevertheless, the speaker goes on to connect her experience to political advocacy and theological authority as the poem ends with a public charge to all Israel to hope in the Lord. The text connects the personal experience of piety with a context of public speech. As we shall see, such public dimensions are common in other poems attributed to women among the biblical texts, troubling a simple dichotomy between male/female and public/private.

One text that troubles such dichotomies is Judges 5, which features the voice of a woman, Deborah, who is a judge, a prophet, and a "mother in Israel." The poem disrupts gendered assumptions, using maternal and domestic imagery in service to political ends. (The Song of Hannah in 1 Samuel 2 employs some similar strategies as well). The poem is somewhat unusual in Hebrew poetry because of its narrative impulse—it tells of a victory in battle. Both Deborah and Barak sing this poem (Judges 5:1), and the voicing shifts back and forth between first- and third-person speech. The public setting is available from the beginning: It speaks of Israelites (v. 2), then turns to address an imagined audience of "kings" and "princes" (v. 3), then addresses God directly ("Lord, when you went out," v. 4), then addresses passersby (v. 10), and then addresses Deborah herself ("Awake, Awake, O Deborah!" v. 12). The cumulative effect of this voicing that turns its face in many directions is the public summoning of all possible available audiences for the remembrance of a great victory.[26] This poem includes details about women and gender, but in almost every case subverts what we might assume to be gendered conventions. Deborah is called a "a mother in Israel," not because she fulfills a nurturing role in the home, but because of her leadership in turning the fortunes of villagers. The decisive moment of military victory is credited to another woman, Jael, whose killing of Sisera is accomplished by a brutal act that is erotic and maternal in its overtones, as well as masculine in its performance:

> Water he requested; milk she gave;
> she brought him curds in a lordly bowl.
> She put her hand to the tent peg,
> and her right hand to the workmen's mallet.
> She struck Sisera:
> she crushed his head;
> she shattered and pierced his temple.
> Between her feet
> he sank, he fell, he lay.
> Between her feet he sank, he fell.
> Where he sank, there he fell—destroyed. (Judges 5:25–27)

The setting of the tent and the provision of milk and bed suggest that the poet is playing with signals of femininity and maternal care. But these are implemented as strategies for battle, which is typically gendered male. The phallic violence of the tent peg and the emphasis on Sisera's ultimate position between Jael's "feet" (a common euphemism for genitals in the Hebrew Bible) presents Jael as a sexualized, genderqueer soldier of sorts, though she does not herself have a voice in the poem.[27] More interestingly in terms of voice, this ambiguously gendered character is framed by the speech of other women. The poem ends with a fantasized conversation between Sisera's mother and her ladies. The mother of the slain warrior is imagined looking out the window and wondering out loud why her once-heroic son is so delayed: "Why do his chariots delay in coming? / Why do the hoofbeats of his chariots tarry?" (v. 28). The answer to her question comes from two sources: her wise counselors (marked grammatically as feminine), and "also, she answers her question herself" (v. 29):

> Are they not finding and dividing the spoil?
> A girl or two girls for every man;

> spoil of dyed cloth for Sisera,
> spoil of dyed, embroidered cloth,
> a dyed cloth, double-embroidered, spoil for my neck.
> (Judges 5:30)

Of course, their answers are wrong. And it is through the multiplication of their voiced mistakenness that the poem achieves its ironic effect. The speakers are excessively coded for femininity: motherhood, the traditional ancient Near Eastern trope of the woman watching at the window, and the grammatical marking of the counselors. The speakers also fantasize about a victory that is coded for femininity, since what the (male) warriors might bring back are "girls" (literally "wombs," *rakhamatayim*), and dyed cloth (typically produced by women). The triplicate reproduction of "spoil" and "dyed cloth" exposes the fixation of these voices, who rightly imagine that the battle follows gendered patterns, but in a twist of dramatic irony, wrongly identify the patterns. They do not know their hero has been vanquished in a complete disruption of their gendered expectations, and what goes unspoken is that these women have already become the "spoil" of another army—a fact not lost on the many publics of the poem's addressees.

In quite a different text altogether, the book of Proverbs also includes feminine voices. Here, the context of the male audience is patent: the whole book is addressed to male children ("my son," Proverbs 1:8, etc.), in keeping with the fact that students in the ancient world would generally have been male. The student's choices between the ways of good and of wickedness are personified by two contrasting alluring women, personified "wisdom" and the "strange woman." This kind of binary thinking is characteristic of the book of Proverbs. Both of these women give poetic speeches, which are juxtaposed in Proverbs 7–8. The "strange woman's" speech is sexualized and predatory: "Come, let us be sated with love until morning; / let us delight ourselves with love. / For the man is not at home; / he has gone on a far journey" (Proverbs 7:18–19). The poem foregrounds the sensual character of seduction, whose voice figures bodily temptation. Personified "wisdom," on the other hand, seems to speak as a disembodied voice, which perhaps contributes to the sense of her authority as well as her spiritual superiority.[28] Like a deity, her voice can be heard but she does not seem to have a physical presence. This feminine voice also seeks out the young men: "Take my instruction instead of silver, / and knowledge rather than choice gold; / for wisdom is better than jewels, / and all that you may desire cannot compare with her" (Proverbs 8:10–11). Her speech develops cosmological imagery, recalling the creation account of Genesis 1:

> Before the mountains had been shaped,
> before the hills, I was brought forth . . .
> When (Yhwh) assigned to the sea its limit,
> so that the waters might not transgress his command;
> when he marked out the foundations of the earth,
> then I was beside him, like a master worker. (Proverbs 8:25–30, excerpts)

Wisdom here is both ancient and closely aligned with the deity. She speaks with divine authority, as a force of life itself. In keeping with the rest of the book of Proverbs, she too addresses her audience as "sons" (Proverbs 8:32). These contrasting women in the book of Proverbs encode virtue and vice in gendered scripts, such that vice is the eroticized feminine, while wisdom is denatured and also powerfully transcendent.

So far, I have considered women's voices in this discussion of gender, because men's voices are so ubiquitous in biblical poetry and women's voices are less familiar to contemporary readers. Of course, men's voices are also gendered. Poems as cultural texts play a role in constructing masculinity, and this certainly factors in our reading and appropriation of them. In "The Song of the Bow," David's poem lamenting the death of Saul and Jonathan (2 Samuel 1:19–27), for example, his language celebrates the military exploits of these two men, securing their place as heroes in Israel, despite that they were defeated and slain. Its repeated refrain is: "How the mighty have fallen!" (2 Samuel 1:19, 25, 27). The voice is a public one that opens with an address to all Israel and calls for rituals of communal mourning. In many ways, this poem's voicing constructs a valiant and violent masculine ideal. At the same time, the voicing shifts in the last lines to a tender reminiscence of a beloved:

> Distress is mine (*li*) for you, my brother Jonathan.
> You were lovely to me (*li*) indeed.
> Your love was wonderous to me (*li*),
> more than the love of women. (2 Samuel 1:26)

These lines echo the sense of deep loyalty and affection we saw in the Song of Songs and in Ruth. As in Ruth, the expression of intimacy does not conform to heteroerotic norms. The repeated *li* "to me" in the three lines underscores the intimacy of the declaration, which stands in some tension with the announced public audience of the mourning ritual. The Song of the Bow valorizes masculine military heroics alongside the language of attachment.[29] Women's voices are not altogether absent from this poem; rather, their voices provide a frame against which the male agents are highlighted: "Tell it not in Gath; / do not report it in the streets of Ashkelon / lest the daughters of the Philistines rejoice; / lest the daughters of the uncircumcised exult" (2 Samuel 1:20). This refusal of feminine public speech is contrasted with the public mourning of Israel's women: "O Daughters of Israel, weep over Saul / who clothed you in scarlet, / with luxury, / who put ornaments of gold on your clothes" (2 Samuel 1:24). David addresses the women and charges them to raise their voices in public acts of mourning. The voicing becomes even more complex in light of the narrative indication that David taught the song to the Judahites (2 Samuel 1:18) and recorded it in "the book of Jashar," a collection lost to us. The voicing, with its multiple and shifting dimensions of address, public and private conflations, and intense emotional exposure paradoxically both reinscribes and challenges its own gendered ideals.

In another example of masculine voicing, the prophet Hosea addresses his audience, which is explicitly identified as male: "Hear this, O priests! / Give heed, O house of Israel! / Listen, O house of the king!" (Hosea 5:1). Provocatively gendered language appears throughout the text, elaborating the metaphor that Israel is like the wife of God. Addressing a male audience as women feminizes and shames them:

> Now I will uncover her shame
> in the sight of her lovers,
> and no one shall rescue her from my hand. (Hosea 2:10)

This technique is seen in several prophetic books (also prominently in Ezekiel, for example). In it, the poet draws on a known image of the city-as-woman. This is a meme that can be seen in literature across the ancient Near East. The personification of a male audience as a city-as-woman, imagining her speaking and acting, is a complex way of offering an explanation for the trauma of destruction and exile. As it does so, it has the effect of both shoring up masculine ideals and problematizing the gendered self-conception of the audience.[30] In one of the most striking examples of feminine voicing in the Bible, Lamentations 1–2 takes up this image of the city-as-woman. The personified city herself speaks:

> Look, O Yhwh, and see
> how abject I have become.
> Is it nothing to you, all you who pass by?
> See, and look
> if there is any pain like my pain,
> which was brought upon me,
> which Yhwh inflicted
> on the day of his fierce anger. (Lamentations 1:11–12)

These are poems that express the grief of the destroyed city of Jerusalem, and outrage against God for the suffering she has endured. These poems use feminine voicing as a counter-testimony to the gendered language of the prophets and implicitly critiques their misogynistic concepts.[31] As a figure, she is presented as the poetic conjuring of a male speaker, who simultaneously speaks about her and for her, and whose voice comes to take full precedence in the third poem: "I am the man who has seen oppression" (Lamentations 3:1). Daughter Zion's voice is full of pathos, but she never quite becomes a full character. While her woeful pleas demand our empathy, she is also a strange figure, her speeches fragmented and disjointed, melded with the voice of the poet. The feminized city is a contested trope in biblical literature, and only in Lamentations is she given a voice of her own.

To talk about voice is different than to talk about authorship. Earlier, I downplayed the significance of authorship in the case of the Davidic psalms, suggesting that the effect of voicing need not have a direct relationship to the text's actual author(s). Certainly, we can almost never be sure about the specific identity of the author of a particular biblical poem. But what about the more general question: Were there women poets? In the case of the Song of Songs, for example, with its style and tenor that differs so markedly from other biblical texts, and which prominently features the voice of a woman, scholars have wondered whether the poetry may be a product of women's culture or a woman poet. It is crucial to take this possibility seriously.[32] The evidence suggests that scribal culture in the ancient world was principally a male domain. But this need not mean that women were not significant producers of culture. There are references to women singing and occasional references to women writing in the ancient world, and in the ancient world as today, "low" forms of cultural creativity—especially in informal and oral traditions—are the paths available to women and those who are otherwise culturally marginalized, who do not have the same access to formal symbolic domains such as writing and publication.[33] In addition, there is evidence in every era of women and men who transgress culturally specific gendered domains of work. So, to ask the question of authorship reminds us of the very real human voices that spoke, sang, and wrote these ancient poems, and as they did so, variously subscribed to or resisted the norms of their own day. As these issues begin to suggest, to ask about gender and poetic voice implies a host of other questions as well, about literary tradition and production, about social roles in the ancient world, about the possibilities of feminine cultures of literary production (oral and textual), about attribution and authorship, access to education, gendered performance, about the ways that gender shapes material experiences, and about the way that gender informs the reading practices of contemporary audiences. To take voice seriously is to see how this poetic dimension opens onto much larger questions about identity and justice.

PSALM 55: A READING

Psalm 55 employs voice as a central technique, and variations in voice serve as a structuring device for the poem. At the same time, the voices of self and enemy are part of the central subject of the poem. The primary voice laments the verbal betrayal of a friend, and the poem's movements will ultimately provide a vehicle for the healing and confident emergence of the speaker's voice. As the voice shifts in tone, address, and content over the course of the poem, it moves through several different configurations of thought that wrestle in different ways with an experience of trauma. The primary voice directs its speech toward God as "you," in the form of a prayer of desperation:

> Give ear to my prayer, O God;
> do not hide yourself from my plea.
> Listen closely to me and answer me.

> I am disturbed in my complaint, and I moan
> because of the voice of the enemy,
> because of the oppression of the wicked.
> For they heap hostility upon me,
> and in anger they attack me. (Psalm 55:1–3)

It is a lamenting poem, though it does not use the typical structure of the lament. (For more on this, see chapter 4.) Instead, the poem's voice shifts in the next lines from these generalized statements about the hostility of enemies to a remarkably interior voice, one that vocalizes trauma:

> My heart writhes within me,
> and the terrors of death fall upon me.
> Fear and trembling come over me,
> and horror covers me. (Psalm 55:4–5)

In verses 6–8, the voice ceases directly addressing God. The speaker in fact momentarily turns away from *any* potential audience and gazes inward. The voicing of the next lines evokes a kind of dream state:

> And I said "Would that I had wings like a dove—
> I would fly and I would rest!
> Look, I would flee far—
> I would lodge in the wilderness.
> I would hurry to find a refuge for myself
> from raging wind and from the storm." (Psalm 55:6–8)

Note how the first word here is *va'omar* "and I said." With this word, the speaker invokes herself speaking. To describe her own voice is to take a kind of temporal and psychological distance from her own self and bodily experience.[34] Looking at herself speaking, she takes us into her interior monologue, into her mind's eye. This imagined journey does poetically exactly what she wishes she could do physically: it momentarily relieves her from the unrelieved, unremitting hostility of the enemies. The catalog of their hostility was four long lines of a single thought. Breaking into that catalog is this image of freedom. The dove in flight soars above the violence below, untouchable. The lines create the poetic refuge that the speaker longs for. But it is only temporary. The next lines take us back into the landscape of prayer:

> Confuse, O Lord, and split their tongues.
> For I have seen violence
> and strife in the city.
> By day and by night
> they go about its walls,
> and wickedness and trouble are within it.
> Ruin is within it.
> Destruction and oppression
> do not depart from its squares. (Psalm 55:9–11)

If the wilderness is an imagined place of refuge, the city is imagined as a kind of prison. It is characterized by a seven-fold description of terror. Violence, strife, wickedness, trouble, ruin, destruction, and oppression are all characteristics of the walled city. While the walls of the city and its guards are perhaps intended to create a space of security, here we find a nightmarish personification. Violence and strife are personified as the guards who relentlessly patrol the city walls, redoubling the conditions from which she cannot escape. The speech of enemy is a grounding concern: "I moan / because of the *voice* of the enemy" (vv. 2–3), and the plea is for an intervention into the enemy's speech: "Confuse, O Lord, and split their tongues" (v. 9).

But the next lines contain yet another striking shift in voice. Now a new addressee emerges. Instead of addressing God or herself, she now addresses a friend. An unusual, repeated dwelling on

the betrayal by a friend resurfaces at several points over the course
of the poem:

> For it is not an enemy who taunts me—I could bear that—. . .
> But (it is) you, a man my equal,
> a friend, and a confidant.
> Together we kept a sweet secret.
> In the house of God we would walk in the crowd. (Psalm
> 55:12–14)

> He stretched out his hands against a friend;
> He violated a covenant.
> His words were smoother than butter,
> but war was in his heart. (Psalm 55:20–21)

These resurgent irruptions evoke the open mesh of trauma, as its
fragmentary memories periodically overwhelm the forward movement of the poem. The effect is recursive, confusing, even chaotic.
This new direction of the voice toward the "You!" of the betrayer
speaks with a sense of rage and outcry, very different from the voice
of prayer. Yet the poem contains them both. Given this wrenching,
interrupting voice of accusation, it is no surprise perhaps that the
poem goes on to call down curses upon the friend-turned-enemy:

> May death come upon them!
> May they go down to Sheol alive!
> For evil is in their dwellings and in their core. (Psalm 55:15)

All of these turns within the poem are shifts in the address of the
individual voice. But there is an even more decisive shift in voicing
later in the poem. At two points, another voice also emerges, who
talks not *to* God, but *about* God in the third person:

> God will hear and he will humble them
> —who is enthroned from of old! *Selah*—

because they do not change,
and they do not fear God. (Psalm 55:19)

Cast your burden on the Lord,
and he will sustain you.
He will never allow the righteous to stumble. (Psalm 55:22)

These lines provide a striking contrast to the voice of the suppli-
cant and offer words of traditional wisdom and consolation.[35] The
assurance given in these lines is essentially that God's justice and
power will ultimately prevail. It sounds like the soothing voice of a
religious authority, as if a priest or counselor were offering support
and advice to a parishioner. It is possible to posit a performance
with actual, separate speakers. Performed in liturgy, one could imagine a choir or liturgist repeating the refrain, "Cast your burden
on the Lord, / and he will sustain you," in the midst of a congregation's prayers of desperation and betrayal. Another possibility is to
see these words as a form of coercion, in which the speaker's pain
is spiritualized and silenced by a voice of authority. Or again, it is
also possible to read this as an interior dialogue, a mind in conversation with itself, offering itself known consolations in the midst
of its distress. Either way, the different voices of the poem enact
a tension between the raw experience of trauma and the voice of
theological assurance.

In cases where distinct voices—even marginal ones—stand
in tension with more dominant or traditionally acceptable ones,
the reader is presented with an invitation to consider how these
voices model the unresolved (and perhaps unresolvable) contest of different voices in dialogue. In Psalm 55, the voice of theological tradition is not given pride of place. Instead, the latter
half of the poem creates a space for it in the midst of its vulnerable, reiterative complaint. But perhaps through the influence of this voice of theological tradition, the individual voice
of the one who prays reemerges at the end with a new sense
of confidence in prayer, orienting its speech once again toward

God, renewing its allegiance to the lament form with a statement of faith:

> As for me, I will trust in you. (Psalm 55:23)

The poem does not ask us to abandon outrage over sin and betrayal. Instead, it creates a space for voicing exactly such feelings. It dignifies them with its particulars of betrayal, even as they stand somewhat in tension with the voice of theological tradition. Here, questions about gender and voice take on a particular poignancy. While there is nothing explicitly gendered about this lament, reading with sensitivity to erotic betrayal and to sexual violence makes this a potent text for contemporary readers. As has been well documented, sexual violence is most often perpetrated not by strangers but by intimates. Betrayal by an intimate, a trusted friend, is all the more devastating when the victim cannot perceive a path of escape, as is often the case for minors and for women in abusive partnerships. Not only the emphasis on betrayal by an intimate but also the imagery and language are suggestive of sexual violence. In other biblical texts, the verb *sabab* "to encircle," which I have translated as "they go about its walls" has sinister echoes. It is used to evoke inescapable terror (Psalms 17:11; 31:13; Jeremiah 6:25), violent military attack (Joshua 6; Judges 16; Jeremiah 4:17), and gang rape (Genesis 19; Judges 19). In Song of Songs 5:7 the men who encircle the city walls strike and wound the young woman after removing her clothes. As in the case of the Song, the imagery here in Psalm 55 has echoes that permit this reading of sexual violence, while not explicitly naming it.[36] While I have used the language of binary gender in this reading, the realities of erotic betrayal are equally possible in homoerotic and queer relationships, and this text can lend itself to readings on behalf of victims and those who are marginalized across a broad spectrum.

Poems like this can give voice to intimate betrayals that are not always accepted or even believed by communities. The betrayal by one "in the house of the Lord" might even be read in light of the clergy sexual abuse crisis. The voices of this poem move from individual trauma to public outcry by virtue of the multiplicity of voices. Here, the more metaphorical sense of "voice," as in "finding one's voice," is particularly appropriate. Poems like this can help readers identify and give voice to their suffering, and to do so with the confidence that God hears the voices of victims and will sustain them.

In another sense, the community created by the poem moves powerfully through time—it has been read and it has given voice to many hearers and readers and reciters over the centuries. As contemporary poet Lousie Glück writes, in her poem "October":

> you are not alone,
> the poem said,
> in the dark tunnel.

The "I" of the lament poem is capable of giving words to our situations, which can serve as a kind of reassurance that we are not alone. In our situations of distress, our own unique "dark tunnel," we are not the first to need or to speak such voices. Glück is a contemporary North American poet, but the idea that the poem speaks for us, as well as assures us that we are in the company of others, is an ancient once. Athanasius of Alexandria (ca. 296–373 CE), in his letter to Marcellinus, remarks about the psalms that they can uniquely help readers find their own voices: "he recognizes [the Psalms] as being his own words. And the one who hears is deeply moved, as though he himself were speaking, and is affected by the words of the songs, as if they were his own songs."[37] For Athanasius, the psalms are a mirror for the soul, which is also what gives them their practical benefit. He sees these voices as useful because they give templates and actions for prayer. On Psalm 55 he writes, after listing many lament psalms and their possible uses, "and if the foes who afflict you hurl insults and the seeming friends, rising up, level accusations at you, and you are grieved in your meditation for a while, nevertheless you also are able to be consoled, praising God and speaking the words of Psalm [55]."[38]

To say that poetry is a mirror to the soul implies a larger recognition about the first-person voice, which is that it invites a particular kind of encounter. As the poem's "I" first mirrors and then becomes the reader's "I" through the habits of reading, the contexts of its creation (who wrote it, and why, and in what situation— questions at the fore in historical-critical biblical scholarship of the last two centuries) become less urgent. The first-person voice so prominent in biblical poetry does not point to a fixed reference, a specific person, but creates the conditions for a moment of encounter and identity. Through this encounter, in which we listen to and recognize the other, the poem becomes a way for readers to find themselves not alone, but in a community of voices.

2

Lines

WORDS ARE THE BUILDING BLOCKS of poetry. How they are crafted together into lines is one thing that distinguishes poetry from prose. The line in biblical poetry tends to be relatively brief. This means that poems are organized around pauses, small ones, perhaps almost imperceptible ones, that hold the space between the turning of one line to the next. This periodic brief pause affects the rhythm of the poem and its temporality. Where the pause occurs in the course of the line's pulse of syllables, accents, and sounds affects what the speaker and the audience hear. This is its rhythm. At the same time, the persistent pause affects time itself. During a poem's reading or recitation, the line will subtly shape the drama of words in time: a long line can stretch out a thought, a short line can create a sense of abruption. And the periodic returning, over and over, to the pulse of the pause itself slows down the procession of thought.

Different languages and literatures have unique types of lineation and rhythm. When they work together in a numerically fixed system, this is *meter*. In its history, English poetry has been a metrical tradition that leans toward iambic pentameter (five beats per line, unaccented-accented: lub-DUB). In French, the Alexandrine dominates (twelve beats, divided into two six-beat parts). Homer and Virgil composed mainly in dactylic hexameter (six beats, long-short-short). In contrast, biblical poetry is not a metrical tradition. It does not develop a style governed by set measures of syllables or accents—though later Hebrew poetic traditions will. Instead of a fixed pattern of beats, stresses, and accents, its lines move with a

An Invitation to Biblical Poetry. Elaine T. James, Oxford University Press. © Oxford University Press 2022.
DOI: 10.1093/oso/9780190664923.003.0003

changing pulse of accents and syllables. It is a fairly free rhythm, though more constrained than contemporary free verse, which has lines that can be super short (one word!) or stretchy and rambling and prose-y.[1] Biblical poetry is generally limited to three to six accents, and four to sixteen syllables or so per line. More often than not, it will have two or three Hebrew words per line. This is hard to see in translation—English often uses far more words than Hebrew—but I will try to make it apparent as much as possible by presenting transliterated Hebrew along with English translation.

Here is a couplet from the Song of Songs, with the Hebrew transliterated. Reading it out loud, you can hear a musicality in the lines, though it is not regularized by meter:

> *tseror hammor dodi li*
> *ben shaday yalin*

> My beloved is to me a bag of myrrh
> that lies between my breasts. (Song 1:13, NRSV)

There is a mellifluous rhythm to these lines in Hebrew. The first dimension of this is the sound-play in the first line (I indicate accents with capitalized letters): *tseROR* and *hamMOR* rhyme, and they have the same number of syllables and accents; *doDI* and *LI* rhyme, but the last word is abbreviated, bringing the line up short. The second line has the same number of accents as the first line, but fewer syllables, so the words feel drawn out with a bit more leisure: while in the first line *tseROR* squeezes two syllables into one beat, in the same beat in the second line, *BEN* gets the full beat. The second line does not rhyme, but *shaDAY* and *yaLIN* blend pleasantly together, beginning and ending with the same sound complement "ay" and "ya." This lends the second line a quiet, fluid quality. This musicality is difficult to replicate in English: the NRSV's "bag of myrrh" does not quite capture it. But the sound of the Hebrew words points up the aesthetically rich sensory experience of the lover's presence. While myrrh is a spice that appeals to the sense of smell, the rhyme evokes its beauty aurally, in a cross-sensory way. The lingering rhythm of the second line evokes the leisure of lovers, who wish to stay mingled in embrace. The point to note here is that the line is heard. It is an organization of sounds. Any account of lineation (in any poem in any language) is a way of describing the experience of words in time, which is a central dimension of a poem's art.

One of the principal ways that biblical poetry enacts rhythm is through a technique of repetition. It is common to find that consecutive lines of Hebrew poetry repeat basic elements. Here is an example:

> The floods have lifted up, O Yhwh,
> the floods have lifted up their voice.
> The floods have lifted up their roaring. (Psalm 93:3)

These lines of Psalm 93 comprise a triplet. The repetition is easy to see. The first two (Hebrew) words of all three lines are repeated: *nas'u neharot* (have-lifted-up the-floods). In this way, both the sense (semantics) and the grammatical structure (syntax) are repeated. It is more common for biblical poems to use synonyms in consecutive lines, rather than direct repetition. The use of synonyms can be seen in lines two and three here: "their roaring" is synonymous with "their voice" from the previous line. In this case, the direct repetition creates a nearly identical rhythmic profile for each of the verses, which nicely mimics the inexorable crashing of waves. The basic fact to observe is that lines use repetition of various kinds, which contribute to the overall character of parallelism.

PARALLELISM

Parallelism has attracted much attention as a (if not *the*) fundamental technique of biblical poetry. There are many scholarly accounts of the varieties of parallelism that the biblical poets employ, which the interested reader may consult.[2] For our purposes, it is

most useful to think about parallelism as a form of repetition at
the level of the line. It is a basic but not necessary feature of biblical
poetry. Consider the following example:

> *bidvar Yhwh shamayim na'asu*
> *uveruakh piv kol-tseva'am*
> *kones kanned mey hayyam*
> *noten be'otsarot tehomot*

> By the word of Yhwh the heavens were made,
> and by the breath of his mouth, all their host;
> who gathered as a heap the waters of the sea,
> who puts in storehouses the deeps. (Psalm 33:6–7)

Biblical poetry tends to be organized in two-line couplets, like these
ones. This is not always the case—one also finds in biblical poetry
single lines, triplets, and quatrains. But more often than not, the line
of biblical poetry is linked to another line. For this reason, scholars of
biblical poetry have often talked about the line having two parts, called
"bicola" or "hemistichs," with a pause, or "caesura," in the middle. It
is simpler to use the familiar language of "line" and "couplet," though
with the reminder that Hebrew poetry generally tends to think
and move through the doubled step of parallelistic lines.

In each couplet here, the word order of the second line of echoes
the first. The second line of the first couplet omits the verb ("were
made"), which is simply implied. In the second couplet, the syntax is
perfectly parallel. Each line begins with a participle: "who gathered"
and "who puts." Each line ends with a watery object: "as-a-heap
the-waters of-the-sea" and "in-storehouses the-deeps," which both
follow this pattern: prepositional phrase + object. The deep orderli-
ness of these lines of poetry evokes the work of the deity at creation,
imagined here as organizing the waters into their domains.

Note that the sentence stretches across all four lines. Its grammar
is additive, and the whole idea of the sentence is not complete until
the last line. This is a key idea for thinking about both the line and

parallelism. Sentence structure can relate in a variety of ways to line structure and to repetition. (This idea will be more fully developed in the section "Enjambment"). One effect of this relationship between the sentence and the line is on the audience's experience of time. Parallelism creates a non-linear experience of time for the audience. Not only are repeated lines memorable because they are repeated, they also temporarily suspend the forward movement of ideas, creating a kind of momentary, rhythmic dwelling. In this example, the first line of each couplet has four accents, and the second has three. But the first couplet contains far more syllables. The line, which limits the length of each clause, constrains the rhythm while it simultaneously slows down the thought.

Repetitions serve memory and recitation, and so it is useful to think of parallelism as a hallmark of an oral-aural poetry.[3] Both the performer (who may or not be the poet) and the audience (who may or may not also be reciting, performing, or singing) are given the space to move slowly, even circuitously, through the ideas of the poem. Something new may be uncovered in each recursive movement. If the point of the poem were merely to affirm God's creative work, presumably a single, straightforward statement would do the trick. As a technique, parallelism implies what is already implicit in the poem-as-art: mere statement of an idea is not sufficient, nor is it the point. The poet asks us to delay the forward charge of ideas and to remain in the experience of the poem. The same suspension occurs when the poem reverses the syntax, as it does in the next lines (I have translated woodenly to make the Hebrew word order more apparent):

Let them fear Yhwh, all the earth.
Him let them dread, all dwellers of the world. (Psalm 33:8)

Here, the second line fronts "him" instead of the verb "let them dread." In Biblical Hebrew, the conventional word order is verb-subject-object, though this is more flexible than in English, and can be varied for effect. While this is not an extreme case, placing the object "him" at the beginning of the line emphasizes its significance. The poets make use of this flexibility, and disruptions to standard word order tend to highlight the fronted word.

In Psalm 107:16, the first line fronts the verb, while the second line suspends the verb to the end, creating a mirror image of the first line in the second (called a "chiasm"):

> For he shattered doors of bronze,
> and bars of iron he severed. (Psalm 107:16)

I will lay it out to highlight the "centering" effect of the chiasm:

> For he shattered (verb)
>   doors of bronze (object)
>   and bars of iron (object)
> he severed. (verb)

Not all chiasms have a special meaning or effect. But occasionally, this kind of variation contributes fruitfully to the poem's overall vision. This is one such case: grouping the two architectural obstacles at the center magnifies the reader's sense of their fantastic heft (and of Yhwh's power to overcome them). And the final phrase, "he severed," is not couched in the center of the line, but effects its closure, evoking the disruptive strength Yhwh's great power.

In some cases, lines in parallel present alternative possibilities or use a contrast to point to a larger, related idea.[4] In the Song of Hannah (1 Samuel 2:1–10) such antitheses are central to the program of divine reversal that the poem envisions:

> The bows of the mighty are broken,
> but the feeble gird on strength . . .

> The feet of his faithful ones he will guard,
> but the wicked in darkness will perish,
> for not by strength does one prevail. (1 Samuel 2:4, 9)

Couplets with contrasting lines such as these are most characteristic of the poetry of the book of Proverbs, especially the memorable two-line aphorisms concentrated in chapters 10–22. Its
poetry is shaped by binary thinking that contrasts good and bad,
light and darkness, wisdom and foolishness, righteousness and
wickedness:

> A fountain of life is the mouth of the righteous,
> but the mouth of the wicked conceals violence.
> (Proverbs 10:11)

> Better a serving of vegetables if love is there
> than a fatted ox and hatred with it. (Proverbs 15:17)

In each of these cases, parallelism is used to expound two potential paths of behavior. In the first example, the line structure is
simple and spare. One idea is presented, and the second idea is
presented in contrast, joined by a conjunction, "but": "the mouth
of the righteous . . . / but the mouth of the wicked." In the second,
the structure is only slightly more complex. Like the first couplet,
it too presents a simple contrast. In this case, though, the syntax
subordinates the second line to the first through the use of the
comparative: "better is a serving of vegetables . . . / than a fatted
ox . . . " The simplicity of the aphorisms, along with their discrete,
autonomous quality, suggest that their ideas are portable and ap-
plicable. They are lessons to be consumed, remembered, and reapplied. This digestibility is aided by the line, which imposes limits
on the units of thought and draws the audience back through its
recursive structure.

   To return to Hannah's song, while the whole poem employs
couplets of opposites to suggest the overturning of the obvious
order of the world, the larger structure is more complex. As we
have already seen, this revolutionary sentiment is not entirely re-
stricted to couplets (note the triplet in 1 Samuel 2:9). More variable

forms can be noted, which build greater complexity into the poem as a whole:

> Yhwh (is) the killer and the reviver,
> who brings down to Sheol and raises up.
> Yhwh (is) the impoverisher and the enricher,
> who humbles; who also exalts;
> who raises up from the dust the poor;
> from the ash heap he lifts up the needy
> to seat them with princes,
> and bequeaths them a throne of honor.
> Surely the pillars of the earth are Yhwh's,
> and he set the world upon them. (1 Samuel 2:6–8)

This section of the poem is bookended with affirmations of God's power to create. The first couplet affirms God's power over life and death. These lines call to mind the deity's structuring of the world. In each couplet of this section, the second line not only repeats the idea of the first line, it also develops it. The general observation "Yhwh is the killer and the reviver" is made more concrete by the affirmation that God "brings down to Sheol and raises up." And again, "Surely the pillars of the earth are Yhwh's" is developed by the second line, "and he set the world upon them," which imagines a process of creative completion. The second line of the couplet complements and develops the first, creating a (very) minimal sense of narrativity. So, parallelism is not merely the simple reiteration of meaning. It can also be used to create subtle dynamism.[5]

A closer consideration of the these lines will show how parallelism is used in different ways. In the first quatrain (four-line section), parallelism is employed across two couplets, neatly coordinating the deity's actions in destructive action (killer/impoverisher) and in constructive action (reviver/enricher). There are two kinds of parallelism here that map differently across the four lines. Semantic parallelism takes place within the couplet (I will use dashes here to show where English uses more than one word for

a single Hebrew word): "Yhwh (is) the-killer and-the-life-giver" ||
"who-brings-down to-Sheol and-raises-up." Each conveys the idea
of death as descent and renewal as ascent—Sheol is the deathly
underworld in ancient Israelite thought. Similarly, in the next two
lines, impoverishment is paralleled by humbling; enrichment by
exaltation. While this kind of parallelism is taking place within
each couplet, syntactic parallelism takes place between alternating
lines, where every other line matches or nearly matches its grammatical elements:

Yhwh (is) the-killer and-the-reviver	(verse 6a)
Yhwh (is) the-impoverisher and-the-enricher	(verse 7a)
who-brings-down to-Sheol and-raises-up	(verse 6b)
who-humbles, also-who-exalts	(verse 7b)

The whole quatrain maps the movement spatially through verbs
of descent (bringing down/ bringing low) and ascent (raising
up/exalting). This spatial movement continues to inform the
subsequent lines:

who raises up from the dust the poor;
from the ash heap he lifts up the needy
to seat them with princes,
and bequeaths them a throne of honor.
Surely the pillars of the earth are Yhwh's,
and he set the world upon them. (1 Samuel 2:8)

The grammar here spills over from the first couplet into the second,
a technique called "enjambment." The sense is not complete until
the verb "to-seat-them" (an infinitive construct) gives a purpose
clause that shows the destiny of the poor. Note, though, how this
enjambment is not terribly radical. No syntax is disrupted, and
each line is comprised of a complete clause. But the full sense of the
whole section is not revealed until the purpose "to make them sit

with princes" is elaborated. Usually, when syntax runs across lines, it is contained within the couplet. It is rarer to see enjambment take place across couplets. So, the enjambment between the couplets here is notable. It contributes, perhaps, to a sense of rising grandeur. On initial reading, the first couplet seemed like a complete thought, but the second couplet extends and revises the idea. Not only are the poor to be raised up beyond their base condition, but God will give them thrones and exalt them with positions of social dignity.

There is nothing in the nature of parallelism that prevents its use over any number of potential domains: word, line, couplet, larger grouping, or even larger stretches of poems. Indeed, the proliferation of forms of repetition suggests its creative potential. In the fable of Jotham in Judges 9, parallelism occurs not at the line level but at the level of subject and stanza. Each plant's action and response follow a set formula: the trees go to the olive, the fig, the vine, and the bramble in succession in their search for a king, and the repetitions heighten the sense of the tragic inevitability of their ill-fated quest. In the following example from Isaiah, repetition is the mobilizing technique, but it is not limited to the couplet. This happens on several levels: the individual words "grass" and "flower" repeat across these lines, four times for "grass," three for "flower." Direct repetition of the phrases "The grass withers, / the flower fades" occurs twice.

> All flesh is grass,
> and all their faithfulness, like the flower of the field.
> Grass withers,
> flower fades,
> for the breath of Yhwh blows upon it.
> Surely the people are grass.
> Grass withers,
> flower fades,
> but the word of our God will stand forever. (Isaiah 40:6–8)

The use of repetition is haunting. The first lines, "All flesh is grass, / and all their faithfulness, like the flower of the field" present a central idea. These are normal line lengths (three to six words). But the repeated motif "Grass withers, / flower fades" employs the shortest possible line length in Biblical Hebrew poetry—only two words each. These can be construed as one single line: "The grass withers; the flower fades," as both JPS and NRSV lineate. But two-word lines are possible in Biblical Hebrew poetry, and this lineation is persuasive because it follows the impulse of the opening couplet, which introduces the poem with two separate lines devoted to grass and flower. Moreover, because the theme of the poem is brevity, the especial terseness of these lines is appropriate.[6] Here, the terseness of the line signals the brevity of annual grasses and flowers, who flourish only for a season and then die.

The further repetition of the entire phrase evokes the cyclical nature of plant life. The poem selectively emphasizes death with verbs of decay: "withers," "fades." In view here is the persistent turning of mortality. Death stalks the living. This sense is fore-grounded in the single line that stands alone: "Surely the people are grass." This serves not so much as an explication of the idea but an insistence on the equally vulnerable impermanence of creatures— whether plant or human. For the Isaianic poet, the only power that stands counter to the forces of perishability and death is God. This effect is realized, in part, by the line. Note that the two lines that refer to God are the lengthiest in the poem. At five words, and four words, they are twice as long as the short lines. Both parallelism and the strategic repetition work together to mobilize this medita-tion on creaturely transience and divine endlessness.

Parallelism is also possible on a more distant scale. Consider the repetition of the phrase "Bless the Lord" in Psalms 103 and 104. The phrase opens and closes both adjacent poems, marking their boundaries. This is a kind of distant parallelism that is not used to bind individual lines together (as in the cases discussed so far) but to bind the two poems together. This liturgical formulation causes the reader to assess the relationship between the two psalms, con-sidering how they are mutually illuminating. The phrase "Bless the Lord" is used six times, twice at the beginning of Psalm 103, and four times near its ending, as the poet calls on the broad scope of angels, hosts, ministers, and works to join in the blessing of God. Psalm 104 also begins and ends with the call, "Bless the Lord, O my soul." The line serves as a thematic link between the two psalms. Psalm 103 draws a distinction between the scope of God's compassion and the fragility of humanity. Psalm 104 elaborates in detail God's power to provide for and sustain the world and its creatures, from the cattle to the young lion to the great sea monster. The repetition "Bless the Lord, O my soul" links the benevolence of divine love and justice with a posture of gratitude for the world that exceeds human power.

ENJAMBMENT

About two-thirds of lines in the corpus of biblical poetry are parallelistic. This means that parallelism—and the parallelistic couplet in particular—is a dominant line structure in biblical poetry. But it is by no means the only one. As we have already seen, single lines, triplets, and other line groupings are also possible, and these can be parallelistic or non-parallelistic. So, it is possible to have enjambed couplets, and parallelistic triplets, and other combinations. Even where repetition is used at the line level, it need not be parallelistic, as in the following lines:

> Catch for us foxes—
> little foxes
> destroying the vineyards.
> Our vineyards are in bloom. (Song 2:15)

Here, there is much that is familiar to the Bible's poetic style: the lines are arranged in couplets; each couplet uses repetition—the second line of the couplet repeats a word from the previous line ("foxes," and "vineyards"); and the lines are mostly end-stopped, meaning that there is a significant pause in the phrasing of the sentence that coincides with the end of the line. But the lines are not parallelistic. Even the end-stopping is not as hard as one often finds in Biblical Hebrew poetry. Rather, the syntax runs over from the second line to the third. In this case, the verb "destroying" completes a sentence begun by "little foxes." The development of the idea of the foxes supplied by this enjambment causes a re-evaluation, introducing an almost sinister dimension into an otherwise playful image of "little foxes." About one-third of biblical poetry is enjambed, in which syntax does not coincide with the end of the line but pulls over the line end to the following line. As will be clear in the next example, parallelism and enjambment need not be mutually exclusive: we see parallelism between couplets, while enjambment works across the lines of the individual couplet. (This is a sort of mirror image of what we saw in Hannah's song, where the couplets were parallelistic, but syntactically dependent on each other.) Enjambment itself can create a kind of suspension, where the completion of a thought is pulled over through the pause of the line's end. In the descriptive poem in Song of Songs 5, this suspension helps create an almost teasing quality, where each line anticipates its fulfillment in the next. The context is the young woman describing her lover to her friends:

> His cheeks are like beds of spices,
> towers of fragrance.
> His lips are lilies
> dripping liquid myrrh.
> His arms are cylinders of gold
> inlaid with gemstones.
> His belly is an ivory tablet
> decked with sapphires. (Song 5:13–14)

In each body-part couplet, the sentence begun in the first line is completed by the phrase in the second line. The enjambment evokes the sense of desire, as the audience waits at the cusp of each line to hear how the speaker will creatively elaborate the initial comparison.

The regularity of the enjambment builds the sense of anticipation that serves the larger structure of the descriptive poem, cultivating a kind of breathless captivation by the lover's beauty. Of course, the first line does not *require* the second line, grammatically speaking. The poem would make sense if it were just first lines, as in:

> His cheeks are like beds of spices.
> His lips are lilies.
> His arms are rounded gold.
> His belly is an ivory tablet.

These are complete sentences, so the line already ends at a marked pause. I make this point to note how different this is from the more radical forms of enjambment that become part of the stylistics of later poetic traditions. Take this example of radical enjambment in twentieth-century North American poet A. R. Ammons' book-length poem, "Garbage":

> whereas a little while later they're quiet at
> hunt or nest: and when during the drying out after
>
> rains the trickle in the ditch bottom
> quivers by a twig-built strait, the
>
> wonder of it all returns, the separations, *ditches?*
> *ditches?* rain? a self?, a self?, being

The selection highlights how dependent the line is on what comes before and goes after. We cannot even know what the subject of these lines are because they plunge us into the middle of a very long sentence: "whereas a little while later they're quiet" (they are speaking of birds). Note too how each line pulls quite forcefully across its end. The grammar demands it: the line endings "at," "after," even "the," all require that we read on to make sense of the line. And the verb of the sentence, "returns," is lodged deeply in a thicket of syntax; we have to go looking for it, or we stumble across it and we are surprised by it. Like the trickle of rainwater in the ditch, which prompts this segment's tiny revelation: "the / wonder of it all returns." For Ammons, this technique works in service of the larger vision of "Garbage," which is characterized by heaped-up images and an additive, never-ending syntactic style that evokes the excesses of late capitalist consumption. This is very different from the style of biblical poetry. This modern example makes it clear that no poetic technique (whether enjambment, parallelism, or any other) is necessarily tied to one particular meaning or effect but can be used in a wide variety of ways.

The poetry of the book of Lamentations uses enjambment more than any other biblical poem.[7] This poetic sequence, written after the destruction of Jerusalem in 586 BCE, gives voices to the profound agony of personal and political displacement and to the terror of war. The poem is composed in couplets, in which the first line tends to be longer (usually three words) and the second line tends to be shorter (usually two words). This long line / short line couplet is very difficult to see in English translation. Many of these couplets are enjambed, as in the following example:

> In the tent of Daughter Zion
> he poured out his anger like fire. (Lamentations 2:4)

This creates a certain fluidity within the couplet. In this example, we have to read forward for the verb, which keeps us attentive across the natural pause at the end of the line. Enjambment does not cause that initial pause to disappear. At some moments, it creates an opportunity for re-evaluating the apparent meaning of the first line. This opens the door for irony, as in the opening lines of Lamentations:

> How! She sits alone,
> the city once full of people. (Lamentations 1:1)

The initial line can be read straightforwardly. A city "sitting alone" is a positive image of security and imperviousness in other texts (e.g., Deuteronomy 33:28; Micah 7:14). The pause at the end of the first line lets the audience sit with that assumption momentarily, before the enjambment pulls us forward and the sense is undercut by the second line. She is not "alone" because she is secure, but because she is gutted of inhabitants after war. The tension between what once-was and what now-is is the fundament of grief that sets the stage for these poems of communal desolation. In these lines, as well as in much of the poetry of Lamentations, the individual couplets are enjambed, while a lack of connective syntax means each couplet stands alone. Most individual couplets come to a hard stop, separating thought from thought and image from image:

> They hunted me (*tsod tsaduni*) like a bird,
> my enemies—needlessly.
> They hurled (*tsametu*) me into a pit alive
> and they threw a stone upon me.
> The waters closed (*tsaphu mayim*) over my head.
> I said "I am lost." (Lamentations 3:52–54)

Only the repetition of the first letter of each of the first words of the couplet (*ts-* in Hebrew) binds the couplets together, as shown in italics. These lines are part of an acrostic (for more on this form, see chapter 3). The isolated couplets hang together on the skeleton of the alphabet, as the poem attempts to hold together community and culture after trauma.

In biblical poetry, the brevity of the line gives poets lots of potential avenues of verbal creativity. How does the sentence and its syntax play against the line? How does brevity itself demand saying more with less? How can repetition be used to different effects? What makes a line, or a couplet, or a poem, memorable? How does it sound? Despite being a fairly traditional body of verse that is keenly aware of its heritage and loyal to its techniques, there are plenty of interesting dynamics at the small scale of the line that show the biblical poets working imaginatively with their art form. In some poems, the line itself becomes a primary way of exploring a theme.

PSALM 19: A READING

Psalm 19 flaunts its poetic crafting, especially through a highly stylized use of lines. The first section of the poem (vv. 1–6) features dramatic cosmological imagery. The word "the heavens," opens the poem with a meditation on the speech of the cosmos. This is followed by six lines about "the sun" (starting in v. 4b). This section uses parallelism in a variety of flexible configurations. Here are the opening lines (the translation is very wooden to reflect the structure of the Hebrew line; read slowly!):

> <u>The heavens</u> tell the glory of God,
> and the works of his hands, proclaims <u>the sky</u>. (Psalm 19:1)

I have underlined the subjects of each line. In each line, these cosmic elements are making a declaration: the heavens "tell" and the sky "proclaims." The syntax of the first line is the reverse of the first (subject-verb-object in the first line; object-verb-subject in the second). The semantic sense of the two lines, the meaning, is synonymous. This neat little chiasm embodies the concern that occupies the first section of this psalm. An act of speech is at the center of each line. What can it mean that the cosmic elements talk about God?

The next couplet continues the meditation:

> Day to-day pours-out speech,
> and-night to-night declares knowledge. (Psalm 19:2)

Here there is a perfect correspondence in the repetition of each element of the couplet: the word order, line length (four words each;

hyphens indicate Hebrew words), and even the meaning are all parallel. Despite the acute parallelism, "day" and "night" are terms with opposite senses. Placing them in parallel creates a sense of totality, indicating the widest possible breadth of expanse (a technique called "merism"). The sense this lends is that every possible dimension of the cosmos—spatially and temporally—continually speaks. This is echoed by the rhythm of the lines. "Day to day" (*YOM leYOM*) is three syllables; "and night to night" (*weLAYlah leLAYlah*) is six. Each phrase contains the same number of accents (two, indicated with all caps), and so the effect is a slight increase in pace in the second line. The lineation creates a pleasing rhythmic cadence.

The rhythm continues to feature in the next couplet. In this case, the poet employs repetition within the line itself:

> There is no speech and there are no words;
> their voice is not heard. (Psalm 19:3)

The two parts of the first line are parallel, and the second clause of the line increases the syllables while the number of accents remains the same.

> *'eyn-'Omer* || *we'EYN devaRIM*
> no-speech || and-no words

The effect is drawn through the second line of the couplet:

> *beLI nishMA' qoLAM*
> not heard (is) their voice

The second line of the couplet repeats the thought and increases again the number of syllables (six) within the clause. Yet it is still the shortest line of the entire section—the rest of the section will move to longer, nine to eleven syllable lines. The effect is an increase in pace and a simultaneous sense of terseness. This structure and rhythm highlight the line. Its straightforward claim, "their voice is not heard," belies the complexity of the idea. It is a second-order reflection on the achievement of the poem itself: the poem urges the reader to perceive the cosmos speaking about God's creativity. It simultaneously acknowledges that imputing speech to the more-than-human world is an act of imagination. There is no "speech," and yet the next lines go on to affirm, "their call goes out."

The next couplet continues the meditation on the speech of the heavens, again employing parallelism, but eliding the verb in the second line of the couplet:

> In all the earth their call goes out,
> and to the ends of the world, their words. (Psalm 19:4)

In this first section of the poem, the steady theme is on speech: every single line contains a reference to words, voice, or pronouncement of some kind. The heavens, by simple virtue of their persistent, daily presence, continually announce the glory of their creator.

The next section of the poem slightly shifts its topic. The sky is still the subject, but the poet narrows to a meditation on the sun itself, in strikingly mythological terms:

> For the sun, he set his tent in them (the heavens)
> which like a bridegroom comes out from his wedding canopy
> and rejoices like a warrior to run his course.
> From the edge of the heavens is his rising,
> and his circuit is to their edges,
> and nothing is hidden from his heat. (Psalm 19:4–6)

These lines are relatively long (eight to twelve syllables each). While some dimensions of parallelism are used (e.g., bridegroom || warrior), there is a much looser sense of repetition. The lines are grouped in triplets, which frequently signal the end of a section or of a poem. The focus on the heavens imperfectly effaces the speaker: two passive verbs signal the human perceiver even as the poem makes the cosmos the subject: the verbs ("is not heard," v. 3 and "nothing is hidden," v. 6) make us ask "heard by whom?" and "who is not hidden?" This serves as a reminder that readers are constantly in the presence of the grandeur of the world that does not require them to observe it.

The most stunning shift in this poem begins in verse 7. In this section (vv. 7–11), the poet moves attention away from the heavens and considers the *torah* (law, teaching). Here, the most noticeable effect is achieved by the lines, which are short, highly parallelistic, and uncommonly ordered (I have added a line space between couplets to make them even more obvious):

> The teaching of Yhwh is perfect,
> restoring the soul.
>
> The decree of Yhwh is reliable,
> making wise the simple-minded.
>
> The precepts of Yhwh are just,
> rejoicing the heart.
>
> The commandment of Yhwh is clear,
> enlightening the eyes.
>
> The fear of Yhwh is pure,
> standing forever.
>
> The judgments of Yhwh are true;
> they are righteous altogether. (Psalm 19:7–9)

The couplets share a symmetrical form: a three-word line ("The-teaching of-Yhwh is-perfect") in the same form (subject-Yhwh-adjective) followed by a two-word line ("restoring the soul") in the same form (participle-object). This slightly longer line followed by the slightly shorter line is sometimes misleadingly called "*qinah* (lament) meter," but it is a fairly common rhythmic shape for biblical poetry. The effect of this highly exact repetition is a sense of confidence. The contrast with the first section is striking: in the section on the cosmos, the poet stretches the uses of parallelism in all kinds of directions; in this section, the poem's hallmark is stability. The first couplet, "The-teaching of-Yhwh is-perfect / restoring the-soul" presents "perfection" or "wholeness" as the qualitative nature of God's *torah*. And the lines scrupulously adhere to form, a kind of poetic enactment of the perfection it espouses. This is all the more the case in the first four couplets, all of which consider how divine teaching (law, statute, precept, commandment) positively affects people's bodies (soul, mind, heart, eyes).

This regulation begins to relax somewhat in the fifth and sixth stanzas, which are still parallelistic but not so strict. We move away from individual bodies to a more generalized affirmation "they are righteous altogether" (v. 9). This opens the gate to an aestheticized but differently ordered grouping of lines:

> *hannekhemadim mizzahav*
> *umippaz rav*
> *umetuqim middevash*
> *venophet tsuphim*

> More desirable than gold,
> or much fine gold,
> and sweeter than honey,
> or dripping honeycomb. (Psalm 19:10)

These two couplets are exceptionally brief, only two Hebrew words each. They foreground two objects of desire: gold and honey. The poet returns us to the human body and its sensory perception. The lines glimmer with the color of gold and honey, appealing to the eye, while evoking other bodily desires, appealing to the hand and the mouth. The simplicity of their brevity creates the sense that their truth is incontrovertible. What is more desirable than gold?

What is sweeter than honey? By the logic of the poem, only the perfection of God's *torah*. This perfection provides a measure and an admonition. Human capacity, subject to error and fault, provides a contrast to divine perfection and might respond to the incentive of rewards like gold and honey:

> Also your servant is warned by them;
> in keeping them is great reward.
> Who can detect errors?
> Clear me of hidden faults. (Psalm 19:11–12)

The final shift in the poem is signaled by two triplets, which accomplish the poem's closure, much as two triplets also signaled the closure of the cosmic stanza:

> Also hold back your servant from arrogant sins.
> Do not let them rule over me. Then I will be perfect,
> and innocent of great transgression.
>
> Let them be pleasing, the words of my mouth
> and the meditation of my heart, before you,
> O Yhwh, my rock and my redeemer. (Psalm 19:13–14)

In this (very wooden) translation, it is apparent how these triplets lengthen the lines and loosen the conventions of parallelism. The word "perfect" (translated "blameless" by both JPS and the NRSV) echoes the description of the law in v. 7, which is also "perfect." The echo in such a highly crafted poem is full of meaning. The poem employs a line structure that contrasts the reliability of divine "perfection" with the more organic and entangled "perfection" that might be achieved by the speaker.

The poem ends with a return to the idea of speech. This was the central theme of the first stanza, where the cosmos bespeaks God's splendor (vv. 1–4). Before, there was speech, but "there are not words." Now, there are definitely words. The poem seems to reflect on the poetic art itself, offering "the words of my mouth" with the wish that they would be pleasing. The entire poem, seen in this light, constructs the human speaker as witness to cosmos and law as imprimaturs of divine perfection. The lines themselves, which bear the weight of these words, are effectively and variably mobilized in service to this theme.

In modern Bibles, one encounters these lines as lineated poetry—they are printed with lots of white space to indicate where the brief lines stop before the end of the page. But traditionally, most Hebrew manuscripts were not lineated in this way. They were written continually across the manuscript page, just as prose was. This does not mean that the lines or the poetry did not exist. The shape of the lines is perceptible when hearing or speaking them. The tight parallelism of the *torah* section of the poem has a markedly different sound and feel from the other sections of the poem. The very fact that the poems were not always written down to reflect the specifics of the line structure makes it all the more clear that the poetic line is more a phenomenon of hearing than of vision. This is a reminder of how close the poem is to the human body. It takes shape in the mouth and echoes through the throat, lungs, and rib cage; part of its pleasure we receive in the ear, all the more so when shared in communities of recitation, where the sound of the poem is the sound of other voices speaking in concert and in the necessary dissent of diverse voices. In Psalm 19, the call of the cosmos that goes out is a "line" (*qav*). The poetry of praise is shared by the embodied experience of the worshipping community in concert with the rest of the world. Even the *torah*, divine teaching, is a reminder of the ways our bodies are bound as creatures by such structures of community and dissent. In the view of this psalm, speaking, hearing, and remembering in patterns shared by the natural world and the law are what give the inarticulate ruminations of the individual (the "meditations of my heart") the possibility of being right before God.

3

Forms

FORMS ARE PATTERNS. BUT PATTERNS in literature can be more than simply shapes to copy; they can also be habits of mind deeply ingrained in language itself, informing every dimension of a work of literary art. As Russian literary theorist Mikhail Bakhtin writes: "The word in language is half someone else's."[1] All speaking, writing, and verbal innovation stands in the porous boundary between self and community. Writers and poets are always borrowing ideas, language, images, and whole structures of poems, creating their work both within and against received traditions. Bakhtin memorably remarks on this tension between tradition and innovation in language: "It exists in other people's mouths, in other people's contexts, serving other people's intentions: it is from there that one must take the word, and make it one's own."[2] Part of understanding any poem, therefore, is understanding the pattern that it takes and the larger body of work that informs it.

Patterns can operate at various levels—line, structure, tone, theme or content, sound or rhythm—that can be used over and over in the production of new poems. So, for example, many elementary school students in the United States are introduced to poetry by way of the haiku. This traditional Japanese form uses several overlapping patterns: lines (there should be three), syllables (a set number in each line: five-seven-five), and theme (often a reflection on the natural world). The pattern itself provides a template or a set of possibilities that generates new poetic production. The sonnet, likewise, has a long formal history in English literature: lines (there should be fourteen), meter (usually iambic pentameter), rhyme

An Invitation to Biblical Poetry. Elaine T. James, Oxford University Press. © Oxford University Press 2022.
DOI: 10.1093/oso/9780190664923.003.0004

scheme (depends on the style of sonnet), and theme (often a reflection on love). The haiku and the sonnet are both relatively strict forms that place constraints on the poem. In these cases, the constraints are tight. In Biblical Hebrew poetry, strong or strict forms such as the haiku or the sonnet do not predominate. It seems that the biblical poets worked with a few loose patterns, and, as we will see, these patterns were relatively malleable. Many such patterns have been identified by scholars attuned to questions of genre. I will talk here about a few of the most common.

TERMS

Before discussing a few of the forms that biblical poets worked with, it is helpful to note that these forms are not generally identified by the biblical authors by specific names or terms. So, if the levels of patterning are not tight, neither is the terminology that the biblical poets and editors used to identify them. There are a few terms that the biblical poets use to describe their poetry, but these do not seem to designate genres of production in the way that "haiku" and "sonnet" (or "limerick," "ghazal," "sestina," and "golden shovel") do.

The most common term for a biblical poem is *shir* "song" or "poem." This term links the oral, performance dimension of ancient poetry with music:

Sing (*shiru*) to him a new song (*shir*);
play skillfully on the strings, with loud shouts. (Psalm 33:3)

Many psalms refer to musical instruments, as this one does. Psalm 150 calls for people to praise God with nine different kinds of instruments. The song (*shir* or *shirah*) itself is not a tidy formal term. It refers to a fairly broad range of types of songs and poetry, including victory celebrations such as 2 Samuel 22 (=Psalm 18; also Exodus 15; compare Judges 5) and denotes prophetic oracles in Isaiah 5 and 23. In the text from 2 Samuel 22, David "speaks" the words of this song, though, of course, elsewhere David is famous for making music, and in many cases it appears that these songs were sung.

Another common term for poem is *mizmor*. This term is translated into Greek as *psalmos*. Since the term is used exclusively in psalm superscriptions, *mizmor* appears to be a technical term for a liturgical poem, just as "psalm" comes to be used in English. Some of the psalms are also "songs," like Psalm 92, which is titled with both terms: "A Psalm (*mizmor*). A Song (*shir*) for the Sabbath Day." But the kinds of poems that are identified by the term *mizmor* include a pretty broad variety: laments, hymns, and songs of praise. So it does not seem to be the case that when a biblical poet began the work of creating a *mizmor* or a *shir*, there was one clear pattern to follow. The terms do not refer to fixed forms.

Another Hebrew word used in reference to poetry is *mashal*. It is often translated as "proverb," but the word's meaning is broader than that. The term is linked to the compressed two-line sayings well-known from the book of Proverbs, for example:

> Hate arouses strife,
> but love covers all sins. (Proverbs 10:12)

Here, we can see a basic formal dimension of this *mashal*-saying: it is framed in a couplet, it presents an antithesis (*hate*, on the one hand // on the other hand, *love*), and its theme is moral (don't be a hater). This is a simple form that is eminently repeatable. The form lends itself to the creation of more sayings, which is evident in the hundreds of such sayings in the Bible. The "proverbs (*mishle*) of Solomon" comprise Proverbs 10:1–22:16, and the first half of this collection (10:1–15:33) keeps the form: most of these short poems are framed in couplets, present an antithesis, and deal with themes of moral rectitude. Here are two more examples:

> Worry weighs on the human heart,
> but a good word gladdens it. (Proverbs 12:25)

> The way of the lazy is a thorny hedge,
> but the path of the upright is paved. (Proverbs 15:19)

The very fact that there are so many such proverbs in the poetry collections of the Bible points to the generativity of the form. This form, though, can take many different shapes. The second half of the "proverbs (*mishle*) of Solomon" (Proverbs 16:1–22:16) groups together sayings that are mostly couplets but not necessarily antithetic. Many of these are still moral in theme, but not all of them:

> The crown of elders is their children's children,
> and the glory of children is their parents. (Proverbs 17:6)

These examples from the book of Proverbs suggest that to some extent, or in some circles, the *mashal* refers to a short poem of this type. From other texts, though, it is clear that the term *mashal* has a broader usage, though it still only refers to poetry. This diversity suggests that while the ancient poets thought of the *mashal* as poetry, they did not necessarily consider it a particular form. Here is an example from Ezekiel 24, in which the prophet utters a *mashal* against "the rebellious house":

> Put on the pot, put it on,
> and pour the water in.
> Gather the pieces in it,
> all the good pieces,
> thigh and shoulder;
> fill it with choice bones.
> Take the choicest of the flock,
> and pile the bones under it.
> Simmer the stew,
> and boil its bones in it. (Ezekiel 24:3–5)

This is strikingly different from the sayings of Proverbs, though it nevertheless shares the setting in short lines and heightening features like soundplay. As is often the case in Ezekiel, the poem centers on a searing, evocative image. In Isaiah 14:4–23, Ezekiel 17:2–10, and in four poems in Numbers 23–24, lengthier poems are each identified as a *mashal* and use figurative language to address a nation. These poems are usually denunciations, though in the case of Balaam's oracles in Numbers, the act of denouncing is ironically thwarted as Balaam is compelled to bless Israel.[3] So it is clear that while the two-line aphorism is a form within the corpus of biblical poetry, it cannot be identified exclusively with the term *mashal*.

Other terms also gesture to genres, but none are definitive, nor are they clearly described or manifested. I will note a few of them here. Laments (discussed later), when they are the utterance of an individual, frequently use the term *tephillah* "prayer" in the poem itself and even in the title, as in Psalm 102: "A *tephillah* of a sufferer, when he was faint, and before Yhwh he poured out his complaint" (see also Psalms 17, 86, 142). But there are also non-lament poems that use the term *tephillah* (e.g., Psalm 84:8). Divine utterances in prophetic poems can be marked with the term *ne'um* "oracle," though this term points more to content than it does to form. And, the term *qinah* "lament/dirge" is clearly associated with poems of lamentation (Ezekiel 27:2; 2 Chronicles 35:25; Jeremiah 9:10). These various examples help us see that the terms ancient poets, editors, and collectors used to describe their work show an awareness of genres, though they were not firmly classifying or theorizing their own work. There is coherence as well as fluidity in their use of terms, which suggests that there may well have been a practical, living oral tradition around the production of poetry. We come to it belatedly, though, and only through texts, so we cannot know it fully.

FORMS

Despite the lack of clear formal terms for poems, there are lots of poems that share recognizable features. These shared features suggest that the poets were working with a known corpus, producing new work in the traditions of the past. There are several recognizable patterns among the psalms, and scholars have spent considerable time identifying various types and subtypes and asking when and how the various forms might have been used in the ancient world. This approach, called "form criticism," was pioneered in the early twentieth century in Germany by Hermann Gunkel.[4] His particular interest was in connecting literary genres to their social and ritual settings.[5] The project sheds a great deal of light on the variety of structural patterns among biblical texts and the psalms in particular. When I use the word "form" in what follows, though, it is not in the technical sense of "form criticism." Rather, "form" is a way of talking about shared literary structures and common features, such as pertain to genres, and the term helpfully retains the important sense that the shape of a text is not separable from its content (unlike the word "structure," for example, which implies that the "poem" exists outside of its particular structural manifestation as a poem).[6] These poems no doubt had some relationship to lived experience, but exactly what this looked like remains speculative. How, exactly, did the ancients use their songs, hymns, prayers, and laments? We can reconstruct some scenarios and practices, but we ultimately cannot know for sure. In what follows, I will consider some patterns available in the texts themselves, and how they serve as both traditions of composition and opportunities for creativity.

HYMNS

The hymn is a familiar poetic form common to the psalter, to other biblical poems, and to liturgical composition after the biblical period (right up to the present moment). Hymns offer praise to the deity. Many biblical praises address God directly, as in Psalm 8, whose opening line is "O Yhwh, our lord, / how majestic is your name in all the earth." The psalm then describes the reasons for praise, including God's creation of the world and establishing humanity's place in it. It ends with the same lines of address with which it began: "O Yhwh, our lord, / how majestic is your name in all the earth." But it is in fact more common that the hymn opens not with an address to God, but with an address to people. Psalms 146–150, for example, all begin with a summons *halelu yah* "Praise the Lord!" and end with the same cry, *halelu yah* "Praise the Lord!" Again, the middle of this sandwich form describes reasons why such praise is due. So, Psalm 146 includes the following grounds for praise:

> Yhwh releases prisoners.
> Yhwh gives sight to the blind.
> Yhwh raises the downtrodden.
> Yhwh loves the righteous.
> Yhwh guards immigrants.
> Orphan and widow he upholds . . . (Psalm 146:7–9)

This particular psalm focuses on the Lord's solicitude for the socially marginalized (prisoners, people with disabilities, those who suffer, immigrants, orphans, and widows) and bases its call for praise in a celebration of God's justice. Psalm 136, another hymn, focuses on the recitation of the saving acts of God, including creation, the Exodus from Egypt, and the giving of the promised land. Psalm 147 lifts up very different dimensions of God's activity and character as warrants for praise. The overall theme is gratitude for the divine support of Jerusalem, but this is linked to a broader awareness of the divine establishment of and provision for the whole world:

> Praise the Lord!
> . . . who covers the heavens with clouds,
> who establishes rain for the earth,
> who makes grass sprout on the mountains,
> who gives to the beast its food,
> to the young ravens when they cry. (Psalm 147:1, 8–9)

The form of the hymn provides a model for celebratory communal speech: start with a summons to praise, describe reasons that such praise is warranted, and end with a call to praise. The very simplicity of the form is part of its appeal. It is replicable. (You could write one right now!) The form also establishes a posture for communal worship—it induces the reader to see herself as one speaker among others. So, the command "Praise the Lord" directs one's speech toward an audience. Because of this directionality, the hymn form is part of discourse that evokes or constructs community. If the reader happens to be reading alone, she must imaginatively address someone or direct that speech internally. Read or spoken in isolation, one could imagine saying the words to oneself: "Praise the Lord." This self-exhortation is explicit in two great hymns, Psalms 103 and 104, each of which is framed by the command "Bless the Lord, O my soul!" (Psalm 103:1, 22; 104:1, 35). The hymn form here is internalized, and the speaker calls herself forth as the community of address.

The poets occasionally seem aware of the way that the hymn form is a discourse that constitutes community. The best example of this is Psalm 148, which uses the sandwich form of the hymn, opening and closing with the summons *halelu yah* "Praise the Lord!" and includes two rationales for praise, in verses 5–6 and 13–14, "for he commanded and they were created . . . " and "for his name alone is exalted . . . " The poet sees fit to radically extend the audience of the call to praise, and the greater part of the poem is given over to naming those to whom it is addressed:

> Praise him, all his angels;
> Praise him, all his hosts!
> Praise him, sun and moon;
> Praise him all stars of light! . . .
> Praise the Lord from the earth,
> sea monsters and all deeps . . .
> Mountains and all hills,

> fruit trees and all cedars!
> Animals and all beasts,
> creeping things and birds of wing!
> Kings of earth and all peoples,
> princes and all judges of the earth!
> Young men and young women,
> old with young! (Psalm 148:2–3, 7, 9–12)

The poem uses the hymn form to constitute a cosmic community. This is not only a command to one's (human) neighbors. To read this poem is to see oneself as part of a larger fabric of creation, in which the individual members—snow as well as stars, trees as well as monsters, wild animals as well as domestic ones—are all commanded to offer praise. The radically expansive sense of community and the techniques that mobilize it—personification and anthropomorphism in particular—will be discussed in more detail in chapter 4. For the time being, it is notable that it is a prevalent feature of hymns that humans name themselves as one among the multiple beings in the universe, all oriented toward a purpose larger than themselves.

Closely related to the hymn form, individual songs of thanksgiving are also a significant form that can be seen throughout the Bible. Like the hymn, they express a sense of gratitude and often relief. One example can be found in the song of Jonah, which is found in Jonah 2:2–9. In its narrative setting, this poem is prayed by Jonah while he was stuck in the belly of a large fish. But the poem itself opens with the conviction that God has already intervened: "I called from my distress / to Yhwh and he answered me" (Jonah 2:2). The irony in the juxtaposition of prose and poem here is that while the narrative would have us expect that Jonah is in dire need of deliverance, the poem recounts its thanksgiving for help that has already been delivered: "You raised up my life from the pit / O Yhwh my God!" (Jonah 2:6). The language throughout the poem is stereotypical—nearly every phrase is traditional, recognizable from other psalms. Like many thanksgiving poems, this one makes reference to sacrifices offered at the temple: "As for me, with a voice of thanksgiving / I will sacrifice to you" (Jonah 2:9). In this way, it calls attention to itself as a liturgical performance.

LAMENTS

While the book of Psalms includes many poems of praise, it is the lament form that predominates. Clustered in the first part of the book of Psalms are poems that are often referred to as "laments" or "complaints"—not because they are identified as such by title or term, but because they share a basic structure, vocabulary, and theme. Scholars have noted that the pattern is quite recognizable and takes the reader through a standard set of movements. These movements are visible in Psalm 13. Here it is in its entirety (the italicized labels are my additions to indicate thematic shifts):

Invocation	How long, O Yhwh? Will you forget me forever?
Complaint	How long will you hide your face from me?
	How long must I bear counsel against me,
	daily sorrow in my heart?
	How long will my enemy rise against me?
Request	Look! Answer me, Yhwh my God.
	Light my eyes, lest I sleep death,
	lest my enemy say, "I have triumphed."
	My foes will rejoice because I am shaken.
Affirmation	But I—in your love I have trusted.
	My heart will rejoice in your deliverance.
	I will sing to Yhwh for he has rewarded me.
	(Psalm 13:1–6)

The Psalm moves through several shifts. It opens with a cry, "How long, O Yhwh?" Psalms of lament typically begin with some kind of address to God, which we see here in the invocation of the divine name: "Yhwh." The opening secures the speaker's place in the presence of the deity. The irony is not lost on the speaker, who though invoking the name and presence of God must bear witness to the experience of divine absence. The speaker seems to feel forgotten by God, whose face is hidden.

In this poem, a series of questions form the complaint, which often makes up the bulk of a lament poem. These lines present the situation of suffering: while God is absent, it is the enemy who is woefully present. Note, though, that while psalms can be quite elaborate in their complaints, which refer to all types of suffering— sickness, anxiety, persecution, betrayal, communal trauma—they are almost always characterized by openness, not by specificity. They do not seem to be the complaints of specific individuals, but rather templates of types of complaint that can be rearticulated and applied to new situations. For example, the "enemy," or "enemies" appear often, but they are rarely named.

A shift happens in the sixth line of Psalm 13, where instead of a question, the line opens with a command: "Look! Answer me, Yhwh my God!" The psalm turns here to its request. It asks something of God, an intervention: "Light my eyes, lest I sleep death, / lest my enemy say, 'I have triumphed.'" The speaker appeals for advocacy, for God to intervene on behalf of the sufferer, enabling them to be vindicated before their enemy. What exactly might such an intervention look like? Again, the lament form prefers to speak in generalizations. In real people's actual lives, asking for God's help might have very concrete dimensions, but the form of the lament tends to keep the purview of God's intervention broad. Again, this openness serves the purpose of re-applicability. Later pray-ers can use the striking metaphor of the psalm, asking for "light" for the eyes in a situation that threatens "death." What does "light" mean? What does falling into the sleep of "death" look like? A pray-er in the depths of depression can speak or hear these lines with as much conviction as one who is suffering physically, where death has a more literal potential. The broadness of the request for divine intervention also encourages a disposition on the part of the one who prays: to ask for relief is to begin to look for it, and to suspect that the divine is already at work to effect change. The openness of the psalms gives the one who prays a similar sense of openness in interpreting their own life as a place where the holy work of healing is imminent.

Finally, lament psalms end with a swing toward confidence and hope. This one concludes with a twofold affirmation. First, the speaker makes a statement of trust: "But I—in your love I have trusted." In spite of the bitterness of the complaint, in spite of being overwhelmed by suffering and threat, the speaker has managed to hold onto security in God's love. The final line then concludes with a second affirmation, this time retrospective: "I will sing to Yhwh for he has rewarded me." It declares that the divine intervention the lament cries out for has already happened. The effect messes with the experience of time: the present is cast in light of the future. The poem asks the speaker to stand momentarily outside of time, evaluating the experience of suffering from the vantage of its relief. The lament form, like therapy, offers a pathway of words before a powerful listener whose presence already begins to signify relief. The form itself dignifies the depth of experienced trauma, and it shapes the articulation of trauma through restoration.

This lament pattern of *invocation-complaint-request-affirmation* is relatively standard, but the shape of the different components can change. (Biblical scholars will note that I am using a simplified paradigm.)[7] In other psalms, the movement toward praise is more elaborated, as in the case of Psalm 6, which ends this way:

> Turn from me, all you workers of wickedness,
> for Yhwh has heard the sound of my weeping.
> Yhwh has heard my plea;
> Yhwh accepts my prayer.
> All my enemies will be ashamed and greatly terrified;
> they will turn and be ashamed in a moment. (Psalm 6:8–10)

That God hears the "sound of my weeping" draws on the image of sorrow at the center of the poem: "I flood my bed all night; / with my tears I drench my couch" (Psalm 6:6). This psalm, though, keeps its eyes firmly on the future, imagining a vindication yet to come. The hope signaled here is drawn out with almost as much length as the expression of complaint. The effect engenders confidence and trust, which are able to counter-balance the felt experience of sorrow. In other psalms, the expression of hope is much more abbreviated, or more tentative, as in Psalm 38. Here, the same lament pattern of *invocation-complaint-request-affirmation* is again visible. And yet the shape of the psalm is remarkable because of how lengthy and virulent the complaint is. The invocation already plunges us into its articulation of despair: "Yhwh, do not punish me in your anger!" and what follows is a multistage description of woundedness and isolation: "For your arrows have sunk into me" . . . "My wounds stink and fester" . . . "My heart throbs, my strength abandons me" . . . "My friends and companions stand off from my affliction" (Psalm 38:2, 5, 10, 11). The affirmation is almost entirely shrouded by the complaint. It peeks out in verse 15, "But it is for you, Yhwh, that I wait; / it is you, Yhwh my God, who will answer," only to be subsumed again by the reemerging cry of woe: "For I am ready to fall, / and my pain is constantly with me!" (v. 17). At the end of the poem, we are left with only a hint of praise:

> Do not abandon me, O Yhwh.
> My God, do not be far from me.
> Hurry to help me,
> O Yhwh, my deliverance. (Psalm 38:21–22)

The request comes only here, a last gasp after the breath is spent in complaint. The final phrase "Yhwh my deliverance" is barely a note of praise—the only one in the entire poem. Psalm 38 plunges the speaker into its despair and hardly surfaces at all. This poem shows how the formal pattern of the lament can be shaped to serve a particular vision of the poet. In this case, the lament psalms' tendency toward praise is implicitly challenged by the poem, which makes complaint most worthy of consideration.

Noting the pattern helps us appreciate departures from it. Psalm 88 is a remarkable lament in this regard. We walk through its early verses and recognize the pattern: *invocation* ("O Yhwh, God of my salvation . . . let my prayer come before you," vv. 1–2); *complaint* ("For I am full of troubles, / and my life draws near to She'ol," v. 3). Then the complaint goes on, line after line, deepening over the course of the next nine verses. But a *request* is hard to find, buried as it is in accusations: "Why, Yhwh, do you reject my life, / hide your face from me?" (v. 14). Even more dramatically, there is no turn to hope or praise, no *affirmation*. Not one word of it. The poem sinks down further and further into its articulation of despair, and the ending simply falls off: "You have made friend and companion far from me; / my neighbors are in darkness" (v. 18). To read Psalm 88 is to drop into a pit from which there is no obvious rescue. Because the form of the lament presses us so insistently, so urgently and repeatedly toward hope, we experience the despair of Psalm 88 all the more acutely. The moral force of this poem lies in the poet's rejection of the form—the utter refusal to be coached or coaxed into praise. If Psalm 38 plays with the possibility that complaint is more pressing and vital than praise, Psalm 88 fully embodies it. Those who brought these poems into the collection noticed, valued, and preserved them and apparently did not see the need to make them conform. This gesture on the part of the ancient curators of biblical poetry quietly maintains a space in the tradition for such voices of dissent.

The laments I have discussed so far have been individual laments. But there are also a number of communal laments in the biblical traditions, which foreground the liturgical context of worship and collective experiences of loss. In some ways they share a communal ethos like the hymn form. These include Psalms 44, 79, 80, and 83, and the poems of Lamentations. The prominent "we" voice in such poems reminds the reader that these poems were written for, and decidedly evoke, the religious experience of a group of people living in a distant time and place. By the force of the poem's voice, and by the re-appropriation of reading, "we" who are reading the poems now also become the "we" that speaks within them.

LOVE POEMS

Love is of one poetry's most quintessential topics across the world and through time. The standout example in the biblical texts is the Song of Songs, but there are occasional allusions to love songs in other texts that gesture to a broader tradition of ancient Hebrew love poetry that is now lost to us. For example, Psalm 45 is called "a love song," and it seems to describe a royal marriage: "You are the most beautiful among mortals; / grace is poured out on your lips" (v. 2); "The princess in her chamber in gold-woven robes is dressed; / in many-colored robes she is led to the king" (vv. 13–14). The fact that "love song" (*shir yedidot*) is in the superscription suggests that it may have been seen as a genre term. While Psalm 45 evokes the scene of a wedding, it does so in the context of praising God. The Song of Songs, on the other hand, does not include specific references to God. Instead, it directly voices desire for the (human) beloved. Part of this erotic imagination can be seen in several poems of the Song that describe the lover's body in list form. Each list is comprised of a series of comparisons. Three of these describe the young woman (Song 4:1–7; 6:4–7; 7:1–6), and one describes the young man (Song 5:10–16). The pattern is simple: each of the lover's body parts is compared to something, moving either from head to toe, or vice versa. Here is the first example:

> How beautiful you are, my friend,
> how beautiful you are.
> Your eyes are doves behind your veil.
> Your hair is like a flock of goats

streaming down the slopes of Gilead . . .
Your two breasts are like two fawns,
twins of a gazelle,
grazing among the lilies. (Song 4:1, 5)

The next poems describing the young woman are quite similar to this one, repeating some of the same imagery, and similarly focusing the lover's gaze on the head and torso. The final descriptive poem (Song 7:1–6) reverses direction, starting at the feet: "How lovely are your feet in sandals!" and then moving up to the top of the head. The form is a list—the catalog attempts to account for the aesthetic experience of being in the presence of the desired other. This formal catalog of features is not limited to biblical poetry; it can also be found in other poetries as well, in both ancient and modern contexts. Ancient Egyptian love poetry occasionally uses the catalog form:

One alone is (my) sister, having no peer
More gracious than all other women . . .
Shining, precious, white of skin,
Lovely of eyes when gazing.
Long of neck, white of breast,
Her hair true lapis lazuli . . .
She has captured my heart in her embrace.[8]

Ancient Mesopotamia, too, sees catalogs of this kind as part of the register of erotic poetry. In the eighth century BCE Neo-Assyrian "Love Lyrics of Nabu and Tashmetu," the goddess Tashmetu is described from thighs to feet: "[whose an]kle bones are an apple of Siman! / whose heels are obsidian! / whose whole being is a tablet of lapis lazuli!" The point here is simply that the catalog is one form that is especially available to and especially evokes the lovers' experience. It becomes a standard genre in later literatures. It is central, for example, to the medieval Arabic poetic tradition. Descriptions of lovers' beauty are also central to the English sonnet tradition, so much so that they become the subject of parody, as in Shakespeare's famous Sonnet 130, which begins this way: "My mistress' eyes are nothing like the sun; / Coral is far more red than her lips' red." Forms, in other words, can transcend time and culture, and they can provide a literary vocabulary that sponsors reimagination in new moments.

PARODY

Parody is one particularly potent form of reimagination. Parody is a way of twisting known motifs to fit new purposes, often by imposing novel or surprising content on a known form. Because the bodies of love poetry in the Hebrew Bible are so limited, we are hard-pressed to identify formal dimensions of ancient Hebrew love poetry per se. But the prophetic use of the language of love suggests that these prophetic poets engaged known forms of love poetry in order to reapply them satirically. This seems to be happening in Isaiah 5. In this poem, the prophet opens with the following line: "Let me sing to my beloved / a love song about his vineyard." Here, the vineyard is a figure for the people (see chapter 4). In the love poetry of the Song of Songs, the vineyard suggests fruitfulness, beauty, and erotic enjoyment:

> Come, my love,
> let us go out to the field.
> Let us spend the night among the henna;
> let us set out early for the vineyards.
> Let us see if the vine has budded,
> (if) the grapes blossoms have opened,
> (if) the pomegranates are in bloom.
> There I will give my love to you. (Song 7:11–12)

In Isaiah, on the other hand, where fruitfulness is expected, there is only disappointment: "He expected it to produce grapes, / but it produced wild grapes" (Isaiah 5:2). The poem gestures to a love poem, developing imagery of care and devotion for six lines (v. 2), then subverts the expectations of the form with a description of regret and impending destruction:

> I will make it a waste:
> it will not be pruned or hoed;
> it will grow over with thorns and thistles.
> And I will forbid the clouds
> from raining rain upon it. (Isaiah 5:6)

The expectation established by the poet's use of the conventions of love poetry is dramatically subverted by the strong tones of judgment and predictions of disaster. In Isaiah 14, the poet parodies another form, the dirge. The dirge is specific kind of lament for a death. One clear example of a dirge form is in David's lament over the death of Saul and Jonathan in 2 Samuel 1:19–27. Isaiah uses recognizable features of the dirge form but to very different ends. Such features include the exclamation "How!" and the opening announcement of death (2 Samuel 1:19; Isaiah 14:4), the consistent use of the three-beat / two-beat lines, and a summons to mourn (2 Samuel 1:24; Isaiah 14:16–17).[9] In Isaiah 14, though, the effect of the parody is humorous—instead of mourning the death of beloved friends and local heroes, it mocks the fall of a tyrant. This "death" does not provoke mourning, but rather speculation about the tyrant's ultimate insignificance:

> Is this the man who made the earth tremble?
> who tottered kingdoms? . . .
> But you are cast out of your grave
> like a loathsome corpse. (Isaiah 14:16, 19)

This poem seems to rely on a known form of lament for the dead, but takes those assumptions and conventions and employs them to satirical effect. There is a certain delighted, vindictive energy in

Isaiah 14 that is accomplished through its use of the dirge form. The pattern provides an occasion for another sort of creation altogether. Once the pattern—any pattern!—is established and internalized, its potential becomes available for further creativity.

ACROSTICS

One of the most formally fixed types among biblical poems is the acrostic. In biblical acrostic poems, the first letter of each line or stanza spells out the twenty-two letters of the Hebrew alphabet in order. This is also called an "abecedarius"—a text that follows the *a*, *b*, *c*'s. Some acrostics in ancient Babylonian literature, as well as many later poems across the world, use the first letters of the acrostic to spell out a name or even a sentence, as a kind of hidden message. (One Babylonian acrostic spells out "I, Saggil-kinam-ubbib the incantation-priest, am adorant of god and king.")[10] There are about a dozen acrostics among the biblical poems, and they do not spell out a hidden message, but all follow the order of the alphabet. To use an acrostic is to call attention to one's membership in a community marked by shared language and shared commitments.

The simplest of the biblical acrostics are Psalms 111 and 112. In these poems, each line begins with a letter of the alphabet in sequential order. These are as spare as the form will allow. One line corresponds to one letter. Here are the *a-b-c* (א–ב–ג) lines of Psalm 112:

(א) Happy is the person who fears Yhwh.
(ב) In his commandments he greatly delights.
(ג) Mighty in the land his descendants will be. (Psalm 112:1–2)

Both the style and the vocabulary are stripped down, and there is not much in the way of contest or complexity. Each line is brief and contains a direct affirmation of faith. These two simple acrostics

(Psalms 111 and 112) are paired, and they are quite similar to each other. The *waw* (ו) line of each is identical: "and his righteousness stands forever" (Psalm 111:3; 112:3). The *khet* (ח) line in each is also nearly identical:

(ח) Gracious and compassionate is Yhwh. (Psalm 111:4)

(ח) Gracious and compassionate and righteous. (Psalm 112:4)

And each of the *samek* (ס) lines starts with a variation on the root *s-m-k* "support." Otherwise, all the alphabetic headwords are different, which begins to hint at how the form fosters creativity in the tension between convention and selection. These poems have a surface-level simplicity that calls to mind the practical tasks of learning the alphabet (and, indeed, abecedaries are known scribal exercises). Their ordered, transparent affirmations of religious faith add to their didactic quality. In Psalm 25, the acrostic form is slightly expanded, to one couplet per alphabetic letter (with the exception of a triplet in the *khet* [ח] stanza). There is a pronounced emphasis on instruction— the verbs "learn," "lead," and "teach" occur with some frequency. Similarly, Psalm 37 is a further expansion of the form, in which the alphabetic letter heads the first line of a quatrain (two couplets). Here is the *aleph* (א) stanza:

(א) Do not be angry because of the wicked;
do not be jealous of wrongdoers,
for like grass they will soon wither,
and like green grass they will shrivel. (Psalm 37:1–2)

The poem moves in this way. The next stanza, the *bet* (ב) stanza, begins with a command to trust, which comprises a quatrain assuring peace and security for those who delight in Yhwh. A stock phrase repeated throughout this psalm is "they will inherit the land" (Psalm 37:9, 11, 22, 29; compare v. 34). Who is "they"? In the vision of this poem, "they" are the righteous, the oppressed, who trust and hope in Yhwh, those whom Yhwh blesses and exalts. The acrostic is a form that evokes this commonsense dimension of the biblical faith tradition, that God will be faithful in caring for those who seek goodness and not wickedness.

In all these examples, the acrostic offers a traditional, even staid, form that declares its allegiances to traditional patterns of wisdom and thought. As Robert Lowth, a notable eighteenth-century scholar of biblical poetry, writes: "The chief commendation of these poems is that they are excellently accommodated to ordinary use; that the sentiments are serious, devout, and practical; the language chaste and perspicuous; the composition neat."[11] It is not surprising, then, to see the form taken up in the book of Proverbs, which is itself quite "serious, devout, and practical." The final poem of the book of Proverbs employs the acrostic in its description of the "worthy woman." This poem uses the acrostic to afford a sense of the totality of the woman's virtues. It describes her hard at work early in the day (Proverbs 31:15) and at night (v. 18); buying (vv. 14, 16) as well as selling (vv. 18, 24); providing for her household (vv. 14, 15, 16, 21) as well as the poor (v. 20); being wise (v. 26) and fearing God (v. 30). The poem layers these totalizing perceptions over the acrostic form, giving the redoubled impression that nothing is missing from the worthy woman's proficiencies. Her virtues are complete. The tidiness of the form provides a firm macro-structure that serves very well for these poems that enshrine practical values like integrity and reliability.[12]

But we need to complicate this picture a bit. As I have suggested—and as parodies in particular remind us—no form's meaning is entirely fixed. Just because a poet chooses the acrostic form does not mean that it will necessarily conform to its historical conventions. This is nowhere more evident than in the book of Lamentations. In four of its five poems, the alphabetic acrostic provides the formal backbone of the poem. This is somewhat surprising, since the texts of these poems are so very different from the other acrostics we encounter in terms of theme, imagery, and tone. Written after the destruction of Jerusalem by the Babylonians in

586 BCE, these poems express bitter outrage over communal loss. Grief and trauma are the thematic center of these poems. Because of their theme, we might expect to see the poet take up the familiar form of the lament, known so well from the book of Psalms. The lament form seems like the perfect vehicle for poems about suffering. While some elements of the lament form do surface in the poems of Lamentations, especially in chapters 3 and 5, the dominant formal structure of the poems is the acrostic. As we have seen, this familiar form evokes order, stability, and traditionalism. So it feels ironic, or at least strange, to encounter the acrostic here.

The irony is available in the very first line. Other biblical acrostics announce the confidence of their subject in the opening *aleph* (א) lines:

> I will give thanks (*'odeh*) to Yhwh with my whole heart
>   (Psalm 9:1)
> I will bless (*'avarakhah*) Yhwh at all times (Psalm 34:1)
> I will give thanks (*'odeh*) to Yhwh with my whole heart
>   (Psalm 111:1)
> Happy (*'ashre*) is the one who fears Yhwh (Psalm 112:1)
> Happy (*'ashre*) are those whose way is blameless (Psalm 119:1)
> I will exalt you (*'aromimkha*) my god (Psalm 145:1)
> A worthy woman (*'eshet-khayil*) who can find? (Proverbs 31:10)

But each of the acrostics of the book of Lamentations opens with something profoundly different:

> How! (*'ekhah*) She sits alone (Lamentations 1:1)
> How! (*'ekhah*) The Lord become an enemy in his anger
>   (Lamentations 2:1)
> I (*'ani*) am the man who has seen affliction (Lamentations 3:1)
> How! (*'ekhah*) The gold has dimmed (Lamentations 4:1)

The opening word of three of the acrostics is not really a word. What I have translated "How!" (*'ekhah*) is more of an outcry than it is a meaningful lexeme. It serves as an index of expression—it could be translated "Oh!" or "Alas!" or "Woe!" or "Ah!" Like a scream or a moan, it stands alone, foregrounding the emotional experience of the speaker. This is a signal of the subversion of the acrostic form. The poems of Lamentations use the alphabet not to affirm the orderly goodness of the divinely structured cosmos, which elicits praise; instead, they use the alphabet to structure the expression of the dissolution of order. Because the first word is almost a non-word, the use of the acrostic form becomes a way for the poet to protest meaning itself.

At the same time, while the poems of Lamentations protest meaning, they also become a way of navigating the loss of meaning and of reconstructing meaning in its wake. The acrostic centers the fundamental bearer of communal meaning—language. In the wake of the destruction of the temple and capital city, and after the experience of successive waves of exile, there is a very real problem of what it could possibly mean to still have a coherent communal identity. So, the poet of Lamentations turns to the shared heritage of language—and the specific heritage of the acrostic as a form of faith—to contain the overwhelming and amorphous experiences of trauma and violence. It strains the acrostic to do this. This why the first word, "How!" ('ekhah), barely a word, feels so strange here: it rips through silence with its protest. In what follows, there is a tension between form and content. The head of each stanza steps purposely forward through the sure steps of the alphabet, and its lines are mostly formally neat, following a fairly regular three-beat / two-beat rhythm. But the imagery is sprawling, forceful, and confusing. The stanzas develop a catalogue of horror:

> (מ) From on high he (the Lord) sent fire;
> into my bones he sent it down.
> He spread a net for my feet.
> He turned me back.
> He left me a desolation,
> ill all day long. (Lamentations 1:13)

(ד) He (the Lord) drew his bow like an enemy.
He set his right hand like a foe.
He killed everything precious to the eye
in the tent of Daughter Zion.
He poured out his fury like fire. (Lamentations 2:4)

Among the evocations of slaughter, havoc, and destruction, the poet has a persistent concern for the human costs of war. The *lamed* (ל) stanza in Lamentations 2 implores the audience to serve as witnesses to the suffering of children:

(ל) To their mothers they say,
"Where is grain and wine?"
while they faint like the slain
in the city streets,
as their life is spilled out
on their mothers' lap. (Lamentations 2:12)

The fact that the poem strains with and against its form is a subject in the next stanza of this same poem:

(מ) What will I say for you, to what will I compare you,
O Daughter Jerusalem?
To what will I liken you, that I might comfort you,
O maiden Daughter Zion?
For vast as the sea is your brokenness.
Who can heal you? (Lamentations 2:13)

Here, the poet acknowledges the fundamental impossibility of writing a poem that could serve a meaningful purpose amid the incoherence of lived trauma. The experience of ruin is "vast as the sea," a figure that gestures to the forces of primordial power and chaos. And yet the poet cannot keep silent: though the experience threatens to overwhelm life, order, and meaning, the poet writes to seek what "comfort" and "healing" there are to be found.

The resources of the acrostic form are the tools for this work. The alphabetic acrostic, a long form, requires thinking forward, with, through, and beyond the immediacy of trauma. Each subsequent letter is like a tiny headlight or a beacon, providing just enough light for the next lines, with the hope that each part will become part of a larger, meaningful whole. It is telling, though, that one acrostic is not enough. If one takes the four acrostics of Lamentations in sequence, there is a sense that the singular iteration simply cannot contain what it is being asked to contain. To put it another way: the alphabet is a complete form. By principle of its existence, it suggests wholeness. All the letters are there.[13] But to use the form to encapsulate brokenness and turmoil, one runs up against the problem of limits. Because the excesses of trauma cannot be contained, perhaps one acrostic cannot be commensurate to the task. As if to underscore this point, the book of Lamentations abandons the acrostic form in its final chapter and ends with a question:

> Why have you forgotten us forever,
> abandoned us for length of days?
> Restore us, O Yhwh, to yourself, and we will be restored.
> Renew our days as of old.
> For if you have utterly rejected us,
> raging bitterly against us—(Lamentations 5:20–22)

By abandoning the form, the poem refuses the closure that the alphabetic acrostic implies. This refusal is furthered by the incompleteness of the final conditional "if," which leaves the ending of the book hanging, "a willful *non*ending."[14] It remains a radically open text.

PSALM 119: A READING

Psalm 119 also takes the form of the acrostic. Like the poet of Lamentations, this poet stretches the form beyond its normal capacities. While Lamentations does this through its radical content, Psalm 119 takes a different tack, pairing conventional content with a radical expansion of the structure itself. This extremely lengthy poem—176 verses—is written in an eightfold acrostic. Each of its twenty-two stanzas is made up of eight couplets, the first line of each couplet beginning with the same letter of the alphabet. Because of its great length, it is worth considering whether it is actually possible to engage in a "reading" of the poem—the elaborate content challenges the reader's or speaker's capacity to keep the whole of it in mind at once. Instead, the poem offers itself as a kind of journey, in which the reader or hearer must move through its stanzas progressively. This is unlike most of the poems of the Hebrew Bible, which tend to be relatively short. It is also unlike the lengthy narrative poems known to us from the ancient world (like the *Epic of Gilgamesh* from Mesopotamia, the *Baal Epic* from Ugarit, or the Homeric epics from Greece). In those cases, the reader can hold the whole in mind through the signals of story, plot, and character. But Psalm 119 declines these conventions. Instead, the elaborate expansion of the acrostic revels in the multiplication of the form as its chief conceit. It is a kind of technical flexing, as the exhibition of formal mastery becomes the central energy of the poem. It is the singular defining feature: there is a minimum of figurative language or imagery, relatively simple vocabulary, and the topic hews very closely to the celebration of *torah* "teaching, law."

The first line announces the program of *torah* piety that will guide the entire psalm:

> (א) Happy are those whose way is blameless,
> who walk in the *torah* of Yhwh. (Psalm 119:1)

This is a very traditional, didactic couplet. It is not a prayer per se, nor is it a hymn that envelops the reader in community. Rather, it is cast as a kind of instruction for the benefit of whoever might be listening. The two nouns structuring these two lines recur dozens of times throughout the psalm: "way" (*derekh*) is a metaphor for a path of behavior, and *torah* can refer to both the laws of ancient Israelite practice and a more general sense of "teaching" or "instruction." With this inaugural couplet, we see the sense of the poem laid out: the path of righteousness is to be followed and celebrated. But what is this path? Interestingly, the psalm, while oriented toward the celebration of *torah*, declines to describe what exactly that is or means. Instead, the poem runs through a series of synonyms for *torah*, one of which appears in nearly every verse of the psalm: "speech," "word," "statute," "commandment," "judgment," "ordinance," "decree."[15] Instead of describing *torah*, the poem simply reiterates its eminence through synonymity. The recurrent use of synonyms gives the poem a repetitive quality, each couplet marked by similar vocabulary and familiar line structure. There is very little enjambment; each couplet is fairly self-contained. In this way the verses have a comparable feel to the couplets of the book of Proverbs. But aside from the acrostic, there does not seem to be an overarching thematic organization.[16] The couplets relate to each other mainly through alphabetic placement and not through the careful development of ideas. The bravura devotion to the form coupled with the deferral of meaning create the experience of an immersive piety that subsumes the reader. To enter into the reading of the poem is to give over one's sense of autonomy.

At the same time, this is explicitly and repeatedly presented by the poem as an experience of happiness. The opening word of the poem is "Happy." Words like "love," "joy," and "delight" are part of the grounding vocabulary the psalm: "I will delight in your commandments, / which I love!" (Psalm 119:47); "I have inherited your testimonies forever, / for they are the joy of my heart" (Psalm 119:111); "Trouble and hardship have found me, / (but) your commandments are my delight" (Psalm 119:143). The "heart" in ancient Hebrew's concept of the body is perhaps not quite as sentimental as our modern one. It is the seat of mind and memory as well as will, so the motif of seeking with one "whole heart" (Psalm 119:2, 10, 34, 58) evokes loyal observance, not just emotion. It is also in the heart where the poet "hides your word" (Psalm 119:11), an image that connotes both memorization and an attitude of veneration. According to this psalm, to treasure the word of God is a posture of affectionate internalization that produces joy. These gestures toward joy signal the psalm's fundamental playfulness. This playfulness emerges now and again, through repetitions and reformulations. In the *tet* (ט) stanza, five of the eight headwords are *tov* "good" (Psalm 119:65–72). While the rest of the poem carefully avoids head-word repetition, in this section the decided, emphatic repetition exuberantly insists on the superabundant goodness the rest of the poem seeks to evoke. Or again, the word *le'olam* "forever" is reiterated several times in fairly close proximity, in verses 89, 93, and 98. The first time, it is a direct affirmation: "Yhwh is forever!" The second time, the speaker matches this incomparability with a statement of devotion: "Forever, I will not forget your precepts!" When it appears again in the next stanza, the poet's hyperbole advances:

> (מ) How I love your *torah*!
> All day long it is my meditation.
> Your commandment makes me wiser than my enemies
> because it is forever (*le'olam*) with me.
> It gives me more knowledge than all my teachers
> because your decrees are my meditation.
> I understand more than my elders
> because I keep your statutes. (Psalm 119:97–99)

In a poem so thoroughly absorbed with traditionalism, in both its themes and its form, the playful reworking of "forever" draws the speaker into divine eternality to such an extent that it undermines the authority it otherwise extols: "It gives me more knowledge than all my teachers . . . I understand more than my elders." The occasional insistence on the authority of personal experience contributes to this tension between received and practical wisdom. This is similar to the tension we perceive between the traditionalism of the acrostic and the delight the poet takes in stretching the form beyond its normal proportions.

In Gunkel's consideration of the psalms' forms, Psalm 119 represents a late poem that mixes genres, not conforming to the recognizable patterns of hymn, lament, and thanksgiving. In his words, this quality makes it a poem of almost "complete formlessness."[17] This is on the one hand true: Psalm 119 has an expansive, meandering quality. Its movements cannot be anticipated. It contains elements of hymn, statements of complaint, and moments of thanksgiving, but it does not conform to any of those patterns in a holistic way. Yet, its rigorous adherence to the acrostic model also suggests a formalism of the most extreme kind. In this sense the poem is not at all "formless." Rather, it is an exploration of how forms—inherited patterns—can be inhabited, played with, and adapted. Forms (of poetry, of *torah*, of various received religious and aesthetic practices) can demand radical acceptance, where the self is relinquished in community. But these forms can also provide a space for radical self-assertion, as when the poet of Psalm 119 declares his independence from and wisdom beyond his teachers. In the midst of the long wandering of this poem, the speaker observes: "Your statues have become my songs / in the house of my sojourning" (v. 54). The "law" here is transformed into song—poetry—which becomes the habitation, the place of belonging.

There are no forms without communities. When poets take up a form, they do so in deference to traditions and the communities that shape and preserve them, or they do so in protest. Or they do both. Forms thus paradoxically represent both constraint and freedom. The traditionalism of biblical poetry foregrounds constraint, which prompts us to ask how the ancients thought about creativity. If we tend to think about creativity as doing something completely new, then biblical poetry might disappoint. Here in Psalm 119, for example, the *gimel* (ג) stanza uses simple and repeating words throughout. Its last two couplets both start with the commonplace particle *gam* "also, even"—not exactly stunning innovation. So the acrostic here seems to constrain creativity. But the form is an occasion for freedom, in that it creates the context and opportunity for new work. In this psalm, this might be most evident in the *samek* (ס) stanza, where the poet reaches for rarified language, studiously avoiding an obvious *samek*-word: *s-p-r* "to recount, write" (in the verbal form) or "writing" (in the nominal form). Or even more strikingly, in the *taw* (ת) stanza, we might expect lines beginning with the word *torah* since it is the central subject of this massive poem, and yet the poet steadfastly avoids it. This reads as a kind of effortful poetic constraint. The acrostic prompts the poet's ingenuity. The creative potential is perhaps similar to the sense conveyed by the command to sing a new song, frequently repeated in psalms of praise: "Sing to the Lord a new song!" (Psalm 96:1; see also Psalms 33:3; 40:3; 98:1; 144:9; 149:1; Isaiah 42:10).

Even the use of an old form, though, insofar as it provides an opportunity for people to engage with artistic traditions in their everyday lives, is a kind of creativity. To sing an old song or read an old poem is also to engage in a creative act. The poems—even the most traditional and formal poems—provide their readers, reciters, and singers with a space for creativity, through the engagement of body, voice, and memory in the creation of new performances and in the renewal of meaning.

4

Figures

POEMS TRADE IN WORDS FORMED in lines, and this diction
and style give poetry its material substance. The pause at the end
of a line becomes part of the distinctive shape of the poem's sound.
These words arranged with their rhythmic pauses take on and mag-
nify the everyday spoken dimensions of language, pushing them
closer to the art of music. Song, of course, is where the word "lyric"
comes from. The connection to music is perhaps most evident in
the book of Psalms, which includes some directions for musical
accompaniment, and which has served as a liturgical songbook
of Jewish and Christian worship. Words and lines, these first two
smaller dimensions of the poem, tend to appeal most directly to
the ear—their sound distinguishes them.

Another fundamental dimension of poetry is the image—the
"picture" that a poem creates. Not all poetry is equally visual, but
a significant portion of the poetry of the Bible develops various
kinds of images.[1] The imagery of biblical poetry, though, does not
tend toward the representative—biblical poems in the main do
not spend the bulk of their energy in straightforward description.
There are a few exceptions to this, including the descriptive poems
of the Song of Songs, which catalog the beauty of the beloved (the
female beloved, Song 4:1–7; 6:4–7; 7:1–6, and the male beloved in
Song 5:10–16). Here is the central part of the young woman's description of her beloved (whose lineation I discussed in chapter 2):

> His arms are cylinders of gold
> inlaid with gemstones.

An Invitation to Biblical Poetry. Elaine T. James, Oxford University Press. © Oxford University Press 2022.
DOI: 10.1093/oso/9780190664923.003.0005

His belly is a tablet of ivory
decked with sapphires.
His thighs are stands of alabaster
grounded on bases of pure gold. (Song 5:14–15)

Note that each part of the body is described in a couplet that begins
by naming a part of the body, "His arms," "His belly," "His thighs,"
and their forms are visualized as precious materials, "cylinders of
gold," "tablet of ivory," "stands of alabaster." In each couplet the
second line develops the image of the body part by pointing to
manufacture: they are "set with jewels," "covered with sapphires,"
"grounded on bases of pure gold." The cumulative sense is to see
or summon her beloved as a statue, formed with precious materials and crafted with aesthetic expertise.[2] This descriptive technique is complemented by a more naturalistic set of images. Verse
15 ends with the claim, "his appearance is like Lebanon, choice as
the cedars," and naturalistic images dominate when she describes
her beloved's face:

His eyes are like doves
beside streams of water,
bathed in milk,
perched at a brimming pool(?).
His cheeks are like beds of spices,
raised beds of perfume.
His lips are lilies
dripping with flowing myrrh. (Song 5:12–13)

Here we see a minute, vibrantly detailed description of the young
man's face. The four-line description of the eyes absorbs twice as
much attention as the other parts of the body, suggesting that she
is fascinated by the animation in her beloved's eyes. They are liquid
(white, like milk), and they are birds "perched at a brimming pool,"
which seems to evoke both the attentive stillness and the flicker-
ing readiness of a bird at rest. The description privileges the visual,

but it is also multisensory, as the cheeks are scented like spice, his lips are flowers, "dripping with flowing myrrh," which evokes the more proximate senses of smell and taste. At the face, the essential vibrancy of the beloved is enshrined through the layering of poetic images. Of course, what the reader comes away with is not a straightforward image of the beloved per se, but rather the cumulative sense of his allure.

While this poem of the Song shows a descriptive image made at some length, it is more common for biblical poems to use brief, local images that control only a line or a few lines. Many of these press toward the figural. (They do not merely represent an object; they create a comparison of some kind). Consider the following saying from the book of Proverbs:

> Gracious words are honeycomb:
> sweet to the spirit, and healing to the body. (Proverbs 16:24)

The image of honey here is brief. It is visual, in that it invites us to imagine a honeycomb and perhaps the rich amber color of honey. Like the image of the beloved's body in the Song of Songs noted earlier, the image has multisensory dimensions, evoking touch, taste, and smell. The image of the honeycomb is already a figure, gesturing elsewhere, to the nature of speech. With one simple metaphor and hardly any syntax to speak of, the equivalence of honeycomb with gracious speech surprises: honey is taken in at the mouth; speech is what comes out of the mouth. The lines conflate production with consumption. Is it the one who speaks well who is soothed by her own words? Or does the one who hears kind words find them sweet? Speaking and listening are imagined as reciprocally sustaining acts with benefits for all members of the exchange. This condensed, muscular energy is characteristic of the short, two- or three-line sayings found especially in Proverbs 10–30. Many of these (though not all) are driven by images. Images can be the spark of poems, igniting their energy, sometimes dramatically.

In keeping with the shifting of voices that can be traced in biblical poems, we also can trace a shifting of images, where several
embodied perceptions bump up against each other in close order.
In Psalm 1, the poem presents the righteous person, who is

> like a tree planted by streams of water,
> which gives its fruit in season.
> His leaves do not wither.
> In all that he does, he prospers.

This is immediately juxtaposed by the figure of the wicked person:

> Not so the wicked—
> Like chaff, the wind sweeps them away. (Psalm 1:3–4)

The poem is a study in contrasts: the sturdy, well-rooted tree is established, watered in its place, flourishing and fruitful. The wicked
are given only two abbreviated lines, which evokes the ephemerality of dry husks, scattered in a moment on a windy day. We begin
to see here, though, that the poem is less interested in developing
an experience of the tree itself than of pressing toward its figural
dimensions—it gestures toward something else, to the righteous
person.

To give another example, the poet of Jeremiah uses a brief
image of a failing brook to describe fear of and disappointment
in God:

> You have truly become to me like a deceptive stream—
> waters not to be trusted. (Jeremiah 15:18)

This couplet follows lines lamenting the prophet's intractable pain,
in which he asks the "why?" questions so characteristic of biblical lament and so psychologically recognizable: "Why is my pain
eternal?" The image of the unreliable stream dramatizes his imagined answer: because God has not been faithful, like a water source

that runs dry. This image capitalizes on the material reality of a region verging on desert, where water sources were and are prized. It also calls to mind the image of the deity, common to biblical thinking, as the one who brings the water to feed agricultural production. Such an idea can be seen, for example, in these lines from Psalm 65 (a text I will return to at the end of this chapter):

> You visit the land and water it.
> Abundantly you drench it.
> The river of God is full of water. (Psalm 65:9)

Instead of affirming God's provision, Jeremiah undercuts the traditional figure. In the speaker's view, God's river is not to be trusted. The metaphor of the failing stream is vivid, and it is also short: after two lines, it does not reemerge anywhere in the poem.

By contrast, the same figure in the book of Job is more elaborate. Here, Job complains about his friends:

> My brothers are treacherous like a wadi;
> like torrential streams they pass away.
> They are dark, with ice at the surface,
> concealing themselves with snow.
> In time they melt and disappear;
> when it is hot, they vanish from their place. (Job 6:15–17)

The image deepens here, adding a sense of seasonal unpredictability. The treacherous ice and snow make it both impossible to judge the water's depth and to cross the surface with surety. But then heat dries it up, and the waters are nowhere to be found. The poem goes further, expanding the scope of the image to include the thwarted hopes of thirsty travelers:

> The caravans turn aside from their path;
> they go up into the wasteland and perish.
> The caravans of Tema look;

the travelers of Sheba hope for it.
They are ashamed because they were confident;
they come to it, and they are disappointed. (Job 6:18–20)

The elaboration of the image dramatizes Job's sense of betrayal. He is not only thirsty, he is also as weary and alone as a traveler in a parched land. Such elaboration is not surprising in the highly ornate poetry of the book of Job.

In the poetry of the latter part of the book of Isaiah, written during the Babylonian exile, the poet tends to work out more elaborate metaphors, and sometimes they are developed over the course of a poem. Water regularly figures as a source of constancy, life, and blessing associated with divine provision:

For I will pour out water on the thirsty,
and streams on the parched land.
I will pour out my spirit on your seed,
and my blessing on your descendants.
They will sprout among the grass,
like willows beside streams of water. (Isaiah 44:3–4)

The poem operates through a series of conflations between the people of Israel and the land and plants. People thirst for water, just as the parched land does; descendants are commonly described as "seed," and here they will "sprout among grasses." The final line returns to the revivifying waters: the people will be like willow trees beside streams. Only one line steps fully back from this web of earthy associations: "And (I will pour out) my blessing on your descendants." This remains sufficiently general, though, that its literal dimension is opaque; it is the figurative dimension that mobilizes its meaning.

The motif of the divine source of water and the related motif of human beings as plants both point to the highly conventional nature of biblical poetry. Biblical poetry is steeped in tradition, and it tends to delight in re-exploring imagery instead of surprising the reader with the unfamiliar. The biblical poets regularly describe human beings as plants (especially vines, trees, and field crops), and vice versa, plants are described in human terms, anthropomorphized as singing, praising, clapping, and even taunting. In the prophets Amos, Hosea, and Micah, plant metaphors serve the poets' critique of economic exploitation. The book of Hosea employs lots of comparisons of this variety. God is water: "(God) will come to us like the showers, / like the spring rains that water the earth" (Hosea 6:3). People are plants, sown, planted, and fruiting: "Like grapes in the wilderness / I found Israel" (Hosea 9:10). In Micah, good people are like good fruit, while bad leaders are both agriculturally unproductive and threatening:

> Woe is me! For I have become
> like a field picked over of summer fruit,
> like the gleanings of the vintage:
> there is no cluster to eat,
> no first-fruit for which I hunger.
> The faithful have vanished from the land,
> and there is no one upright who is left. . .
> The best of them is like a brier,
> the upright, a thorn hedge. (Micah 7:1–4)

Among the prophetic collections, Isaiah has a particularly rich lexicon of the natural world, with the most diverse vocabulary of plants among the prophets. People are compared to grass (5:24; 66:14), and blossoming is a frequent metaphor, both as a promise of future healing and as a signal of judgment (17:11; 18:5; 27:6, etc.).[3]

This is not to suggest that there are no innovations in biblical imagery, of course. When an image is novel, then the reader has more work to do to establish the connections. For example:

> Your sayings are proverbs of ashes;
> your defenses are defenses of clay. (Job 13:12)

Here, Job chastises the discourse of his friends after having listened to their first cycle of poetic speeches. The image of speech as "ashes" evaluates their worthlessness and calls to mind ephemerality, destruction, and death. This is further mapped by an association with war: their arguments are described as "defenses" (*gabbe*), which is a word that evokes the back of a person or the convex surface of a shield, and casts their dialogue as a battle, which also threatens death. Speech, imagined in terms of emptiness and worthlessness, has the potential to destroy or to crumble slowly, like weak clay in the mortar of a city's defensive walls.

METAPHOR AND SIMILE

Two of the most common figures are metaphors and similes, as in many of the previous examples. These techniques operate by way of comparison: "Your word is a lamp to my feet" (Psalm 119:105); "I am a worm and no human" (Psalm 22:6); "The Lord roars from Zion" (Amos 1:2). Metaphors ("my beloved is a gazelle") and similes ("my beloved is *like* a gazelle") are both types of comparison. What the simile makes explicit—likeness—is assumed by metaphor. In the third example, the comparison itself is implicit: God is a lion, which is how he can "roar." All of them operate with the same basic strategy, which is to imagine one thing in terms of another. This is what Aristotle classically describes as a transfer (*Poetics* 21, 1457b). In comparing the beloved to a gazelle, the metaphor transfers the qualities of the gazelle to the lover. In metaphor theory, these are referred to as the "source" and "target," or "signifier" and "signified."[4] In this case, the reader is invited to imagine a host of qualities associated with gazelles (the source/signifier), which might include grace, litheness, and beauty, for example. These qualities are transferred to the beloved (the target/signified), who is now transformed in our perception. We perceive the grace, litheness, and beauty of the beloved, who is both familiar and strange to our perception as a result of the metaphor. Part of poetry's art is in creating resemblances that ask us to see the world in new ways. What would it mean to see one's lover as a gazelle? The poem invites us to imagine.

In a text from the prophet Micah, the layering of metaphors suggests the power and totality of what is being described. The deity's arrival on the mountaintops will be so magnificent and cataclysmic that the poet stretches for language to describe it: "The mountains will melt under him, / and the valleys will split open / like wax before the fire, / like waters pouring down the steeps" (Micah 1:4). Wax is the signifier; the mountains the signified. It is unsettling to map such an unstable element as wax onto the ancient solidity of a mountain, which we tend to take for granted as examples of stability and endurance. The metaphor of wax also requires us to think of the deity as a raging fire. The poem does not rest, though, with the image of melted wax: it layers on the more powerfully rushing unpredictability of flowing waters. What qualities of the deity are we asked to imagine now? What kind of being can reduce the towering mountains to rushing water? The poem, in layering its metaphors in such a way, stretches the imagination.

But the account I have given is too simple. The resemblances that the poetic juxtaposition creates are in fact quite unpredictable. To return to the example from the Song of Songs: while grace, litheness, and beauty are some of the qualities one might associate with gazelles, and ones that may be particularly suitable for thinking of one's beloved, there are certainly others as well—quickness, shyness, elusiveness, or their penchant for destroying gardens. The associations the poet has put into play are not finally under the control of the poet. Rather, the meaning will also depend on the life experience of the reader, who may or may not have first-hand knowledge of the source or the target. This problem is particularly acute for ancient texts, which are foreign in time, culture, language, and place. There is a certain archaeology of the image that may be required: a little research shows that the roe deer, once the most widespread variety in the eastern Mediterranean, was a very small, shy animal that lived mostly in forest cover. The description is not so much one of majesty (which the English translation "stag" [JPS, NRSV] mistakenly implies) but rather of solitude and secrecy, emphasizing the lover's swiftness and subtlety. Such knowledge will help the reader appreciate the metaphor and give the most generous reading possible to the poem.

This by no means implies that there is one "correct" meaning of a metaphor. On the one hand, it is true that the biblical poets sometimes explain their metaphors to us. The poetry of Ezekiel in particular, which develops the most extended metaphors, tends to explicate them:

> And the survivors who survive—
> They will be in the mountains like doves of the valleys:
> all of them moaning, each over his sin. (Ezekiel 7:16)

How are the survivors like doves? The poet tells us: because they will be displaced and moaning over their sin. Especially in the case of Ezekiel's highly imagistic poetry, a powerful image is elaborated, and then given an interpretation, usually in prose. But such explanations cannot finally contain the energy of an image; even in cases where the explanation is given, the image itself gets pride of place. Sometimes the image remains autonomous, never fully explained. Consider the following lines:

> A sword, a sword—
> sharpened and polished:
> sharpened for a terrible slaughter,
> polished to flash like lightning. (Ezekiel 21:9–10
>   [Heb. 21:14–15])

In this poem, the principal technique is the inexorable repetition of the image of the sword, which is "sharpened and polished," "polished and grasped," "sharpened and polished." In point of fact, the word "sword" is repeated eight times in six verses. Here are several more lines:

> Strike hand to hand.
> Let the sword fall—twice, thrice.
> It is a sword for slaying,
> a sword for great slaughter.
> It surrounds them
> in order to melt hearts,
> and many will stumble.
> At all their gates I set
> the point of the sword.
> Ah, it is made as lightning,
> polished for slaughter. (Ezekiel 21:14–15 [Heb. 21:19–20])

The energy of the poem is in the fixation on the sword's preparation for war. This type of metaphor is sometimes called "synechdoche," where a part stands in for the whole. In this case, the singular sword represents the whole army of Babylon. But the poem's power is in the fearsome image of the gleaming sword, poised to fall "twice," "thrice," the repetition of the image presaging the repeated strike of the blade in hand-to-hand combat:

> A sword, a sword:
> drawn for slaughter,
> polished to consume, to lightning. (Ezekiel 21:28 [Heb. 21:33])

The point of the poem in this case is not simply the "message" that Babylon is preparing for war; rather, it is the nightmarish image of the weapon that is electrically charged and left buzzing in the brain of the reader. It is as though the speaker is taken up in fascination, held by this alarming image, entranced by its horrible, glimmering, beauty. This is a macabre art, one that evokes the despair of victims, who cry and wail, who melt and stumble. A really effective metaphor will lodge in the memory like an unanswered question.

PERSONIFICATION AND ANTHROPOMORPHISM

Once the poem has put the source and the target, the signifier and the signified, together, the image itself is active and alive, and it can become unstable or at least untidy. The close relationship between the terms may imply a fluidity in influence, so that the comparison also flows in the reverse direction. To return once again to the more placid Song of Songs, which likens the beloved to a gazelle, and a mare among Pharaoh's chariots, note: the comparison cannot simply be reduced to the prosaic claims, "my lover in some ways reminds me of a gazelle," or "there are some things about a horse that selectively apply to the person I admire," points that can be dropped as soon as we "get" the desired dimension of the comparison. Instead, the comparison has a redoubling effect, so that everything on either side of the "is" is connected. To say the lover is a gazelle also has the unexpected result of asking readers to see a gazelle with the affection one might have for a lover.

The kind of kinship inspired by such comparisons to the natural world has profound potential for thinking ecologically. It requires a kind of imagination to see the links between humanity and the more-than-human world. This is one ethical potential of biblical aesthetics. Biblical poetry frequently uses personification to develop the reader's empathy for the rest of the creaturely world. Personification (also anthropomorphism) is the technical name for the kind of metaphor that endows the more-than-human world with human characteristics.[5] This device can be seen in the Psalms. Psalm 148 is a striking example (discussed in chapter 3). Another example is found in Psalm 96, in which elements of the more-than-human world have the capacity of speech:

Sing to Yhwh a new song.
Sing to Yhwh, all the earth . . .
Let the heavens be glad, and let the earth rejoice;
let the sea and what fills it roar;

let the field and all that is in it exult.
Then all the trees of the forest will shout
before Yhwh, for he is coming,
for he is coming to judge the earth.
He will judge the world with righteousness,
and the peoples with his truth. (Psalm 96:1, 11–12)

Land, sea, fields, trees, and hills are all imagined as offering praise to God, and, the end of the psalm suggests, they will also be subject to divine judgment. While God is elsewhere certainly described as being enthroned more specifically on the praises of Israel (e.g., Psalm 22:3), the frequent evocation of the praises of creatures and elements suggests a way of thinking about the interwoven and interdependent praise of all of creation.[6] The technique of personification in biblical poetry's expansive conception of praise dignifies the place and, perhaps, even the personhood of the larger created order. The poem becomes site for exploring the perception of the world as inhabited by a wide variety of animated subjects—both human and nonhuman.[7] It is a notable feature of biblical poems, and hymns in particular, that they regularly imagine elements of the natural world praising the deity. It is remarkable that every instance of the natural world "praising" occurs in the poetic texts of the Hebrew Bible, and the majority occur in hymnic psalms and in the latter part of Isaiah, which has commonalities with hymnic materials. The praise of the natural world is clearly a poetic topos that engenders a kind of ecological mindset (before the era of "ecology" as we know it).

One also encounters personifications of the built environment:

Lift up your heads, O gates,
and be lifted up, O ancient doors,
that the King of glory may come in. (Psalm 24:7)

This device features especially prominently in texts of lament. In poetry of destruction, the gates of Zion are said to mourn (Isaiah

3:26; Jeremiah 14:2). We find it, too, in the poetry of deepest dread. To say that roads grieve, as in Lamentations 1:4, is not merely to charge the roads with emotion (though it certainly does that). It also reaffirms a commitment to cultural vitality, to insist that what has been built once may yet have life left in it, though it has been destroyed. Lamentations also takes up the image of the personified city, Daughter Zion, and portrays her suffering with pathos:

> How! She sits alone—
> the city once full of people!
> She has becomes like a widow,
> who was great among the nations!
> The princess among the provinces
> has become a vassal.
> She weeps bitterly in the night,
> and her tears are on her cheeks;
> she has no comforter
> among all her lovers;
> all her friends have dealt treacherously with her;
> they have become enemies. (Lamentations 1:1–2)

To look at a city that has been destroyed by military incursion is to think of the many people whose lives are in disarray or decimated. This correspondence evokes empathy for the communal identity that has been wrecked by the violence of war. The personified figure links personal trauma with political fate. But again, the comparison has a certain untidiness. The city is like a woman, but the city is also elders, young girls, princes, mothers, uncontainable by the idea of the singular suffering. The language hovers between the literal and the figurative. To press this point further, and to return to the example from the Song, to say "my lover is like a gazelle" is also to insist on the gulf of difference between the lover and the gazelle, such that the "is" will simultaneously ask us to perceive both likeness and unlikeness. Because of course the lover is not a gazelle, and in many (or perhaps most) ways is not at all like a gazelle. The imaginative work of metaphor takes place over a gap of difference, and so it will always be dynamic, unpredictable, and interpretive.

METAPHORS FOR THE DEITY

The imaginative dimension of metaphor, and the gap of difference between the elements of the metaphor, have particularly striking repercussions for language about God. Metaphors for the deity pervade biblical poetry. At the same time, biblical poets wrestle with the metaphorical dimensions of speaking about God:

> Who is like Yhwh our God,
> who is seated on high,
> who comes low to look
> on the heavens, and on the earth? (Psalm 113:5–6)

The idea that something or someone could be "like" God is rejected through a trope of incomparability. The poet pointedly refuses to compare God to anything. Think about one creative route the poet could have taken in this poem but chose not to: the poem could have included answers to these questions, various examples of who or what God is like. Instead, the poet resists metaphors, and the questions are met with silence. This prompts the audience to affirm God's incomparability. The implicit answer is: No one! Nothing is like God! God is known in this poem not through figures, but through the affirmation of God's compassionate care for those on the margins of society:

> He raises the poor from the dust;
> from the ash heap, he elevates the needy,
> to seat them with princes,
> with the princes of his people.
> He brings the barren woman home,

a joyful mother of children.
Praise Yhwh! (Psalm 113:7–9)

Psalm 113 participates in one thread of discourse about God in the Bible, which argues that God cannot be properly spoken of. No one can see the face of God and live; even Moses only sees the back of God (Exodus 33:20–23).

But this stands in tension with the variety of imaginative metaphors for God that show up in biblical poems.[8] While many people are familiar with language that speaks of God as "father" (which is quite uncommon in the Hebrew Bible, but which comes to prominence in the Christian New Testament and subsequent theological traditions), they may be less familiar with the host of diverse images that biblical poetry employs in its speech about God. Psalm 18, for example, presents a vibrantly imagined theophany, a revelation of divine presence. It opens with an outpouring of metaphors:

I love you, Yhwh, my strength.
Yhwh is my rock, and my fortress, and my deliverer;
my God, my crag, I take refuge in him;
my shield, and the horn of my salvation, my stronghold.
(Psalm 18:1)

The accumulation of images develops the sense of God as a place of refuge and power, but its technique is minimalistic: there is one verb ("I take refuge") but otherwise there is simply a series of images, each of which is marked by the personal suffix "my" -*i*: "my rock," *sal'i*, "my fortress," *metsudati*, "my deliverer" *mephalti*, to cite only the first three. This is true of all eight nouns used here to describe God. Thus the imagery of insurmountable strength rings with the affirmation of the personal. The strong walls are marked and contained by the speaker's "I" even as they are imagined to encompass and to protect the speaker.

This affirmation of God's deliverance of the individual frames the poem, which makes a very personal plea for divine intervention.

But the imagery of God's appearance moves in the direction of the meteorological and cosmic:

> Then the earth shook and quaked,
> and the foundations of the mountains shuddered
> and shook, because he was angry.
> Smoke went up from his nostrils,
> and devouring fire from his mouth;
> coals from him burned.
> He bent the heavens and came down.
> Thick darkness was under his feet.
> He rode on a cherub, and flew;
> he swept on the wings of the wind.
> He made darkness his shroud,
> his canopy around him dark waters,
> clouds of the skies.
> From the brightness before him
> the clouds crossed:
> hailstones and coals of fire.
> Yhwh also thundered in the heavens,
> and the Most High gave forth his voice.
> He sent out his arrows, and scattered them;
> he flashed his lightning and routed them.
> Channels of water appeared,
> and the foundations of the world were laid bare
> at your rebuke, O Lord,
> at the blast of the breath of your nostrils. (Psalm 18:7–15)

The imagery here is fantastic in scale and mythological in impulse. The appearance of Yhwh is like an earthquake or a storm. God, in anthropomorphic form, has nostrils, a voice, feet, a mouth, and rides on a terrible monster: the cherub was a hybrid creature, described by Ezekiel as having wings and the faces of four different creatures. This boundary-crossing figure signifies the throne of God—where the division between earth and heaven is transgressed. The natural world in the imagination of this poem is summoned to upheaval by the mere breath of this powerful deity. The poem issues a sobering reminder of the fragile status of humans in the larger world.

This contrast between human frailty and the strength of God is further developed through metaphors of God as a divine warrior, who "trains my hands for war, / so that my arms can bend a bow of bronze" (Psalm 18:34). Such imagery sees divine vindication in military victory, so that the speaker moves from a state of liminality, with which the poem begins:

> The cords of death surrounded me;
> the torrents of wickedness terrified me;
> the cords of *She'ol* entangled me;
> the snares of death confronted me. (Psalm 18:4–5)

To a state of surety, with which the poem ends:

> The Lord lives! Blessed is my rock,
> and may the God of my salvation be exalted! (Psalm 18:46)

The poem itself is a study in how the metaphorical imagination mobilizes the praise of the speaker: to read the poem is to enter into its experience of God, and perhaps to allow oneself to be moved from despair to affirmation. This may or may not entail an acceptance of the poem's terms. One might rightly resist the militarizing dimensions of this language for the deity (and its political mismatch with the contemporary context) while acknowledging how this ancient way of talking about God maintains the sense of divine advocacy and power.

Many more metaphors for God abound in the Psalms: God is a shield, a judge, a stronghold for the oppressed, a king, "my chosen portion and my cup," and a bird with sheltering wings. God is a shepherd, who cares for the flock. It is appropriate to note that while Yhwh was conceived as a male deity in ancient Israel, this did not mean that the ancient poets avoided imagining God in other terms. God is imagined in human terms (anthropomorphized) in a variety of ways that create dynamic links between humanity and the deity. God is imagined with titles of governance like king, judge, and lord, as well as with metaphors of service like shepherd, vinedresser, and warrior.[9] Somewhat more sparingly, these texts use kinship language that reflects human intimacies, spouse being the most prominent among them, but also that of parent. This is a recoverable theological contribution of biblical poetry: to enrich language for God with a more inclusive lexicon.[10]

A number of texts use specifically feminine figures for the deity. Psalm 22, a wrenching and lengthy Psalm of lament, affirms trust in the deity who has the skill and compassion of a midwife (a quintessentially female office in the ancient world):[11]

> For it was you who took me from the womb,
> who entrusted me to my mother's breasts.
> It was on you that I was cast from birth;
> from the belly of my mother, you were my God. (Psalm 22:9–10)

The soaring poetry of Isaiah 49, full of the hope and promise of a restoration for exiled Israel, imagines God as attached to Israel as a nursing mother is to her child:

> Can a woman forget her nursing child,
> or show no compassion for the child of her womb?
> Even these may forget,
> but I, I will not forget you. (Isaiah 49:15)

Feminist readers have rightly pointed out the necessity of recovering images such as these.[12] And yet to simply add feminine images to the predominantly masculine ones is not entirely satisfactory, and readers will want to examine problematic or obsolete images. One way to begin is by acknowledging these diverse metaphors for God, which helps underscore the necessary partialness of language for a deity. Occasionally, the poems themselves can be seen to destabilize the gender norms they apparently inscribe. For example, the Song of Moses is one of the few texts of the Hebrew Bible that figures God as father: "Is he not your father, who created you? / He, who made you and established you?" (Deuteronomy 32:6). But the metaphors shift quickly to the animal kingdom:

> As an eagle stirs up its nest,
> and over its hatchlings it hovers.
> It spreads its wings, takes them up,
> and carries them on its pinions;
> Yhwh alone guided him (Israel);
> no foreign god was with him. (Deuteronomy 32:11–12)

This is a rather extended metaphor for a biblical poem, elaborating for several verses the care and feeding of Israel in the desert by this great bird of prey. This shift to the obviously metaphorical eagle should itself serve as a reminder to readers that the "father" language is not literal, either. The poem is working with a patchwork of metaphors. Then the poem shifts yet again, to images of birth, in which God is metaphorized as a mother:

> The rock that bore you, you neglected.
> You forgot the God who birthed you. (Deuteronomy 32:18)

The image of the rock giving birth is arresting, and it too reminds the reader of the necessarily metaphorical dimensions of speech about God. It also underscores the limits of the language of binary gender. God cannot be defined in simple terms of "male" or "female." The mixed metaphor of the gestating rock complicates fatherness by transgressing or subverting categories of gender and sexuality, not to mention species and elements. The poem exploits the gap between the signifier and the signified. It foregrounds God's transcendence while maintaining that the experience of divine provision is understandable in terms of human care.

To take a single metaphor for God too literally, to collapse the distance between signifier and the signified, would be idolatry. This is the concern that seems to motivate the resistance to metaphor in Psalm 113, which rejects the possibility of comparing anything to God. At the same time, metaphors are powerful and necessary for theological discourse, as they give the language that makes the divine available. There is a tension, in speaking about God, between God's transcendence and God's availability. Biblical poems navigate this tension in different ways. Metaphors are their compass.

SYMBOLS

Like metaphors, symbols ask the reader to think of one thing in terms of another. Unlike metaphor, however, a symbol asks the reader to see what has not been said. Metaphor and simile tend to be completed within the poem: in the case "my lover is like a gazelle," both the signifier ("a gazelle") and the signified ("my lover") are named. Symbols can be thought of as a "signifier" in which the signified remains outside of the text—the reference is hidden or opaque or not named. The burden is on the reader to complete the figure, acting on the hunch that the thing in the poem means more than it means. For example, the rose has a long history in the Western literary tradition. When readers encounter a line like William Blake's "O Rose thou art sick," they might have the distinct sense that the rose is not just a rose. It gestures to something bigger. With a minimal amount of cultural knowledge, the reader might infer that the symbol gestures to sexual love—in this case, love that is thwarted or corrupted in some way (it is "sick" and, we find out in subsequent lines, it is "destroyed" by the "the invisible worm").

But the speaker does not tell us what the rose is: it is a symbol. While the rose itself is not a standard symbol in biblical poetry, these ancient texts have their own register of symbols that mean more than they mean.

The following example from Micah employs a couple of related symbols that are relatively straightforward:

> So night it will be for you—without vision,
> and darkness for you—without divination.
> The sun will set over the prophets,
> and it will be dark over them—the day. (Micah 3:6)

In Hebrew, the lines front the sensory terms "night" and "darkness" in the first two lines and the verbs "set" and "be dark" in the second two lines. In this way, the poem accents the symbolic experience of the absence of light. Each line suspends the explication until the end of the line, so we learn belatedly in each case that it is the lack of "vision," "revelation," and "the prophets" that will result from God's withdrawal. This withdrawal is exemplified in the final line, where all indications of these modes of divination are entirely absent, and the poem settles into the totality of the symbol. The day will be darkness. The syntax of the final line suspends the subject (the day) until the last word. Where the previous lines condition us to expect to hear something about divine communication, the absence of any reference to divine communication in the final line is deepened symbolically by the darkness of the day. Later in Micah, the same imagery is put once again to symbolic use: "If I sit in darkness, / the Lord is a light for me . . . He will bring me out to the light" (Micah 7:8–9). If darkness symbolizes a withdrawal of the divine presence, the inverse symbol of light signifies a conviction about divine presence. Radiance evokes hope.

In a poem from First Isaiah, the prophet derides the people for their foolishness and lack of understanding using language of drunkenness (Isaiah 28:7–13). Then, the poet offers a promise using the symbol of a stone:

> Therefore thus says the Lord God:
> see, I am laying in Zion a stone,
> a tested stone,
> a precious cornerstone,
> a firm foundation. (Isaiah 28:16)

What is the "stone"? The reader may be tempted to leap to answer this question, to close the gap between the signifier and the signified. But the poem is not so eager. The text gestures toward this hope, offering the sense of stability and trust that a solid foundation stone implies. It supplies a contrast to the "refuge of lies," which will be swept away (Isaiah 28:17). But the poem holds back the referent. It refuses to answer the question, "What is the stone?" This means the audience must probe its possible meanings.[13] The point of the poem is not necessarily to sleuth out the correct answer, as though the symbol were a riddle to be solved. Instead, the reader is positioned in dialogue with the poem. At the symbol's prompting, the reader must ask where a solid foundation can be found in a world in which public discourse and religious leadership are as confused as though drunken, and "all tables are filled with filthy vomit" (Isaiah 28:8). That solid foundation—whatever it is—is the manifestation of God's justice (v. 17). The symbol in this way offers an invitation to the reader.

As the poem goes on, the coming of God's message is depicted as an anticipated terror. Here, another symbol emerges:

> For the bed is too short to stretch oneself out,
> and the covering too narrow to wrap oneself up.
> (Isaiah 28:20)

In the night of a raging storm, the one who seeks security will be left cold and desperate. But what does the bed symbolize, exactly? A paltry refuge or protection? The ultimate vulnerability of mortals? The insufficiency of human culture? The underworld itself? Any of these is possible. The image is provocative and not finally determined. In cases like this, where a figure strikes the reader as especially perplexing or resistant to interpretation, it is perhaps best to take a step back, and to consider that the questions the poem prompts are as important as their answers. In light of the larger poem, which deals with the false security of those who have made a "covenant with death," the bed conjures a sense of fleeting and false security. It is a bed that is "too short" and a blanket that is "too narrow," and so neither can offer protection from the overwhelming flood of divine wrath that is to come. The contrast between powerful flooding waters of divine justice (Isaiah 28:17) and the insufficient refuge prompts the reader to ask: What "beds" of false security might the ancient audience have been clinging to? Here, commentaries can help fill in some backstory from historical context. The certainty of the Assyrian military advance is in the backdrop here, as is the futility of Judah's attempts to resist by making an alliance with Egypt. But, given that the poet had every opportunity to name such historical dimensions, and yet chose not to, we must take the gap between signifier and signified to be significant. Why might the poet have been reticent to name them? How does this not-naming create provocative ambiguity? Part of the power of the symbol is in what it refuses to relinquish. The deferral of the signified serves as a reminder that the poem needs its readers; it is not complete without them. To hear a poem, and to think with it, is to practice attentive empathy. This requires a willingness to slow down and listen for something not yet fully understood. The symbolic dimension of a poem, perhaps more than any other dimension, asks the reader to approach the text as one might approach an encounter with another person: as a voice that speaks across time, about matters of utmost importance, in a language that we cannot fully understand, in language that might be unresolvable.

At the same time, it should also be emphasized that the final point of a symbol is not necessarily obscurity. Because they are figures that gesture beyond themselves, symbols can be quite conventional and stylized by their very nature. (The rose exemplifies this conventionality.) There are plenty of times in the biblical corpus that the symbolic gesture has a relatively clear referent, even though it goes unnamed. In these cases, it is the audience's familiarity with the symbol that enables them to complete the figure. Some stylized symbols in biblical poems include Daughter Zion (a personified symbol for Jerusalem, discussed earlier in this chapter) and flooding waters (a symbol for primordial chaos that is regularly evoked in traditions about creation and the Exodus).

Since ancient Israel was a settled, agrarian economy for most of its history, it makes sense that some of its most prominent symbols are drawn from the life experience of agriculture. The book of Deuteronomy, describing the inviting potential of the promised land, cites its quintessential crops: it will be "a land of wheat and barley, of vine, and fig, and pomegranate, a land of olive oil and honey" (Deuteronomy 8:8). Within this landscape, viticulture (vines, grapes, and wine production) has a prominent place, in part because of the vine's success as a crop in that environment, and in part because of the durability of its finished goods: wine can be stored for years, transported in jars, and enjoyed well into the future. It therefore becomes an important export commodity. As it serves a significant role in the lifeways of the ancient writers, it also comes to serve a significant role in its literature, in particular as part of its self-imagination. Having one's own vine and fig tree becomes a symbol for self-sufficiency and political peace (Isaiah 36:16; Micah 4:4). Symbols can be images that accrete meaning through consistent and frequent use.

This accretive meaning can be seen with the vine, which comes to mean more than it means. Through its widespread use, it signifies not just agricultural fertility but also the close association between people and land. The vine's health (or unhealth) is a poetic barometer for the health (or unhealth) of the people who cultivate it. Hence the Psalmist's blessing:

> Your wife is like a vine
> fruiting within your house.
> Your children are like olive shoots
> around your table.
> Thus will a man be blessed
> who fears Yhwh. (Psalm 128:3–4)

This association is especially useful for the prophets, who are most adept at speaking in a symbolic register. At times, its meaning is made explicit, as a metaphor:

> Israel is a plentiful vine
> that yields its fruit. (Hosea 10:1)

But other texts rely on the audience's imagination to supply the signified. There is overlap, in this way, between metaphors and symbols. Jeremiah writes:

> I would surely gather them, says Yhwh,
> (but) no grapes are on the vine,
> nor figs on the fig tree,
> and the leaf withers.
> What I gave to them they passed over. (Jeremiah 8:13)

In the context of the larger poem, Jeremiah uses a variety of animal and vegetable images to cast aspersions on his audience's (lacking) moral compass. These culminating lines ask the audience to imagine the painful realization of a failed harvest. The vines are there, but there are no grapes. Other texts that mobilize the symbol of the vineyard include Isaiah 5, the Song of Songs, and Ezekiel 17.

Ezekiel's poem includes a prose interlude that explains his use of the symbol in historical terms (vv. 11–21). But the symbol refuses to be contained by its explication. It seems that resolution can only come through poetry, and so the text ends with a return again to verse (vv. 22–24). The explanation is not enough; the poetry overruns it.

The symbol of the vine also appears in Psalm 80, but this uses the standard figure to somewhat different effect:

> A vine you brought out from Egypt.
> You drove out the nations and you planted it. (Psalm 80:8)

In short, two-word lines, the poem supplies a brief recounting of God's transplanting a vine, with a run of imperfect verbs that give the passage the quality of a tale:

> You turned its surface,
> and it rooted its roots,
> and it filled the land. (Psalm 80:9)

There is no explicit linkage between the signifier and the signified. Instead, the audience must supply the interpretation. Because the vineyard is a well-known symbol for Israel, and more narrowly, for Israel's dependence on God's benevolent care (figured as vine-dresser), the audience might expect to find a poem that defends the deity's care for Israel and perhaps to meditate on human guilt. But this text resists any explanation for destruction. Instead, there is only a wrenching description of the vineyard's abjection:

> Why do you breach its walls,
> that all who pass by on the road gather (its fruit)?
> The swine of the woods raze it,
> and all that creeps in the field graze on it. (Psalm 80:12–13)

The poem is punctuated with a refrain, slightly modified each time it appears: "O God restore us! / Make your face shine, that we may be saved!" (Psalm 80:3; 7; 19; see also v. 14). The symbolic register of the vineyard implies a need for the powerful vision of the sun, which might both apply its powerful heat to burn the enemies (vv. 17–18) and restore to health a broken vineyard. The plant's susceptibility to the energy of the sun is part of the symbolic dimension of this image.

One final example will help to show how a symbol relies on the reader's knowledge of a much bigger world beyond the text itself:

Hope deferred makes the heart sick,
but a tree of life is a fulfilled desire. (Proverbs 13:12)

In this proverb, the "tree of life" is a metaphor for fulfilled desire. But it clearly means more than it means. This excess of meaning is possible because the text evokes a rich world of cultural knowledge. In the iconography of the ancient Levant, trees are sometimes depicted as or with a goddess, sometimes providing sustenance from her breasts. The tree motif suggests divine sustenance. In Mesopotamian texts, a tree stands in the sanctuary of the god Enki. The tree of life is typically situated within a "garden of paradise," or a sacred grove near a temple, and thus is also associated with fertility.[14] While some biblical traditions were suspicious of sacred trees (e.g., Deuteronomy 16:21; Isaiah 1:29–31), others saw them as a source of divine presence or teaching (e.g., Genesis 13:18, 21:33; Joshua 24:26; Psalm 1; Ezekiel 47:12; Proverbs 3:18). The use of the image here associates positive dimensions of desire with the tree, which it envisions as sustaining and fulfilling, and even divine. Symbols understood in this way are points of contact to a world beyond themselves. The broader worlds of the poem will be the subject of chapter 5.

PSALM 65: A READING

Psalm 65 is remarkable for its rich metaphorical imagination. It is a psalm of praise in which not just humans, but the whole of creation is imagined offering praise to God. The poem moves from relatively subdued metaphor to extravagantly imagined personification of both God and the land at the poem's end.

The poem opens with a meditation on speech and liturgy:

> To you, silence is praise, O God in Zion.
> To you, a vow is performed, O hearer of prayer.
> To you all flesh comes. (Psalm 65:1–2)

The opening lines place the reader in the context of temple worship, locating God in Zion and as the one who hears prayer. The first line, which I have rendered "Silence is praise," is often translated "Praise is due" (NRSV) or "Praise waits for you" (JPS), but these translations stem from interpreters' discomfort with the unusual figure of silence as praise, not from the text itself.[15] Already there is a tension: If silence is praise, then what does God hear? How is silence praise? In the next section, speech takes center stage:

> Words of iniquity are stronger than me.
> Our sins, it is you who forgives them.
> Happy is the one you choose and draw near
> to dwell in your courts.
> May we be satisfied with the goodness of your house,
> the holiness of your temple. (Psalm 65:3–4)

The lines begin "words of iniquity are too strong for me." "Words" (*divre*) can also mean "deeds" and is often given this sense in translation. But "speech" makes sense given the interest in speech already in the poem. And the psalms often point to speech as a source of sin. This suggests one possible reason that silence is praise: because human speech is susceptible to corruption.

The poem problematizes human speech, and then goes on to describe the speech of the more-than-human world:

> With wonders you answer us in righteousness,
> O God of our salvation,
> who is the trust of all ends of earth and the wide sea,
> who establishes the mountains in his strength—
> he girds himself with might!—
> who silences the roaring of seas,
> the roaring of their waves,
> the uproar of peoples.
> They fear your signs, those who dwell at the ends (of earth);
> The gateways of morning and evening shout for joy.
> (Psalm 65:5–8)

Here, the imagery becomes more vivid. Several lines evoke tumult. The scope of God's activity is worldwide, and God "silences" the chaotic loudness of both the elements and the peoples. The imagery evokes God's power and blurs the boundaries between human and more-than-human. The earth and sea trust in God, which is a subtle personification. The dawn and dusk open their mouths and shout, which is a bolder personification. All the creatures—human and more-than-human—are subject to God's power. But it is only the landscape that speaks. As humans fall silent, the poem intimates, they might notice that the dawn and the dusk, the east and the west, are "shouting for joy."

The final section shifts to a portrayal of God as a farmer. While the metaphor "God is a farmer" is not made directly, the parallel is implicit in the descriptive imagery of God "watering," "enriching," "smoothing," and "blessing" the land:

> You visit the land and water it;
> you enrich it abundantly.
> The river of God is full of water.
> You establish their grain for thus you establish it:

> drenching its furrows, smoothing its ridges;
> with showers you melt it, its sprouting you bless. (Psalm
> 65:9–10)

This imagery presents God as the source of agricultural bounty, while human farmers are nowhere to be seen. This suggests that while people necessarily undertake the physical tasks of agriculture, they do not create the abundance they reap. The larger, mysterious forces that create abundance remain hidden to the human eye. They are visible only to the anthropomorphic imagination that detects God at work.

In the final lines, the imagery becomes its most extravagant, and the personification of the land comes into full focus:

> You crown the year with your goodness,
> and your wagon-tracks drip with ripeness.
> The wild meadows drip;
> with joy the hills dress.
> The pastures wear flocks,
> and the valleys deck themselves with grain.
> They shout out, they even sing. (Psalm 65:11–13)

Here at the end, the land's "shouting" and "singing" provides a counterpoint to the silence at the psalm's beginning. While human farmers and human praise are invisible and inaudible, the poem revels in personification: The year is "crowned," the hills "dress," the pastures "wear flocks," the valleys "deck themselves with grain," and all the landscape "shouts" and "sings." The poet explores the likeness between humans and the natural world through the figure of personification. While human speech is viewed with some suspicion, the speech of the more-than-human world is celebrated.

The whole psalm pivots around the perceived likeness between humans and the natural world and their capacity to speak. The way the poet does this is through vivid imagery and metaphor. The poem ends with the affirmation that the land "even *sing*[s]," a clear echo of the title of the poem itself, which is a "*song*." The poem's ending loops back to its beginning, signaling yet again the likeness between people and the natural world. The world calls forth human creativity, the making of art, and so while the poem commends human silence, it cannot keep it. The impulse of the verbal art of poetry speaks even about the necessity of its own silence. Susan Stewart writes, "Something continues to call for art, something in the experience of those who make it and something in the experience of those who seek to apprehend it. Nature produces beauty without human intervention, but not artworks, and no artwork can be completed without reception."[16]

In his writings on the psalms, Augustine in the fourth century reminded his audience that "similes can never be perfectly adequate," a readerly sensibility that calls for both humility and creativity. He writes cheerfully, "You do not find this particular image helpful? Very well, take another."[17] There is an implicit appeal here for artful reading and artful writing. If we need not take any particular image too seriously, we must also always be seeking more metaphors, better language, acknowledging at once the imperfection of human speech about the divine and its deep necessity. The task of making figures is never complete.

5

Contexts

SO FAR, THESE CHAPTERS HAVE foregrounded features largely internal to the poems. Features like voice, line structure, and imagery are visible at the surface level of the text and can be discerned and described as aesthetic artifacts. But the reality is, of course, much more complicated. No text exists in a vacuum or is generated out of nothing. Every text is written in a language, is part of a larger conversation, and responds to and participates in a larger world. So, you will have probably noticed a bit of sleight of hand in the foregoing chapters. In almost every one of the previous discussions, the poem's engagement with the larger world has already been evident. This is particularly the case in the explorations of forms (chapter 3) and figures (chapter 4). Given forms remind us that the ancient poets are working in a distinct cultural register, and their speech patterns necessarily emerge from and are shaped by a world very different from our own. Figures in various ways also emerge from historical and cultural milieus, and symbols especially remain incomplete within the poem. They gesture beyond themselves, both back into the world from which they emerge and forward, into the future, toward the reader. The sleight of hand, of course, is the idea that we can simply talk about "the poem" without always already engaging a larger world (and this is true not just for poems but for texts of all kinds). In this chapter, we will discuss a few of the many ways that readings of poems can be enriched by seeking to understand how they are shaped by various dimensions of context.

An Invitation to Biblical Poetry. Elaine T. James, Oxford University Press. © Oxford University Press 2022.
DOI: 10.1093/oso/9780190664923.003.0006

THREE WORLDS OF THE TEXT

While potential contexts proliferate, overlap, and are difficult to untangle (as will become clear), I will discuss here three types of context using a simplified paradigm loosely based on the ideas of French philosopher Paul Ricoeur. Ricoeur talks about the process of interpretation as a development from the event, to the textualizing of the event (writing), to the interpretation of that text. These three stages belong to three different "worlds": the world behind the text, which includes the historical factors that gave rise to it and the author(s) who wrote it; the world of the text itself, which includes linguistic and stylistic questions, as well as the relationships among texts; and the world in front of the text, which is where we—readers—are, shaped by our own myriad contextual complexities and concerns.[1] The reading of any poem is shaped by multiple contexts. In Ricoeur's view, recovering the intention of the author ("behind the text") is impossible because it is a matter of psychological speculation. Instead, he argues that the texts have an ultimate "semantic autonomy," a life beyond their originating context, in which much depends on the engagement of readers.[2] I am sanguine, especially in the reading of ancient texts, that the more we can bring to bear from our knowledge of the ancient world, the more we can create conditions for generous, thoughtful readings. But as we shall see, poems have a way of traveling, taking on new lives in the worlds of different readers. In what follows we will consider how all three worlds—behind, within, and in front of the text—bear on biblical poems.

To take a very brief example, consider Psalm 66. For the most part, the poem speaks in general terms about the praise it seeks to elicit: "Shout for joy to God, all the earth" (v. 1); "At the greatness of your strength your enemies cringe before you" (v. 3). As we have seen before, such open language is characteristic of many psalms, making them interpretable for later readers in ever-shifting contexts. Nevertheless, there are dimensions of the world behind the text that can be noted and explored here. First, the notations

themselves point to liturgical use, for example the repeated word
selah (vv. 4, 7, 15), which is left untranslated. While we do not
know what *selah* means, it seems to be an instructional or musical
notation. Its presence implies a community of liturgical use. This
sense of the liturgical context is heightened by the direct address
opening the psalm:

> Shout for joy to God, all the earth!
> Sing the glory of his name;
> Give the glory of his praise.
> Say to God: "How awesome are your works!
> At the greatness of your strength your enemies cringe
>   before you.
> All the earth worships you,
> and they sing to you, they sing your name." *Selah*
> (Psalm 66:1–4)

These lines assume the voice of a leader addressing a community.
The verbs are plural imperatives, offering directives for verbal
praise. The text gives some clues, then, that help us begin to posit
its use among ancient worshippers. The references to animal sacrifices later in the poem also gesture to distinctive ancient religious
practices: "I will come into your house with burnt offerings. / I will
pay you my vows . . . I will make an offering of bulls and goats"
(Psalm 66:13–15). In order to explore these dimensions of historical context, the reader might turn to other textual traditions
that describe such practices or explore the archaeology of ancient
Levantine temples and altars, for example. In such ways, the poem
reveals itself to be deeply shaped by a historical context "behind
the text," whose dimensions are broad, and which we can begin to
reconstruct through a variety of methods that take us beyond the
poem itself. Such pursuits of historical contexts are the rich legacy
of academic biblical scholarship since the Enlightenment.

   The more the reader presses at these ever-expanding questions
of context, though, the more they seem to proliferate and the more

difficult it becomes to solidify one sure "context" of interpretation. Consider again Psalm 66: the body of the poem goes on to evoke God's saving actions of the exodus: "He turned the sea into dry land; / they passed through the river on foot" (v. 6). This evocation might be understood as referring to something "behind the text"— to a memory of a salvific event. But when one begins to raise the questions of historical context, their dimensions are expansive and slippery. We cannot know, for example, what this exact event looked like or how the text corresponds to or diverges from the actual experiences of ancient peoples. We do not know who wrote the text, or when, or what their situation and audience were. There is a certain inexhaustibility to the question of historical context.[3] This is a necessary quality of historical research: the past is not merely given; rather, it must be hypothesized and constructed in the present after careful selection of evidence. Our knowledge is always incomplete. Nevertheless, some attempt to understand the world from which the poetry of the Bible emerged is necessary. It is one way of navigating the poem's alterity. The poem, while we utter it with our voices, is not ultimately ours. We must ask: What acts of imagination and empathy are necessary as we build an increasingly complex sense of the text?

Psalm 66 also reveals how the evocation of the exodus belongs not only to the world of the past, but it also belongs to the world of the text, as it exhibits relationships to other texts and traditions. Though the story is told in the book of Exodus, the "exodus tradition" is also well-known among diverse biblical texts of different periods, and these texts engage the stories in diverging ways. References to slavery in Egypt and God's self-identification "I am Yhwh your God," for example, appear in other texts like Deuteronomy and the narratives of Joshua, 1-2 Samuel, and 1-2 Kings. Other psalms, too, evoke the exodus tradition, as for example, Psalm 78, another psalm that focuses on retelling events of communal memory: "He split the sea and brought them through it. / He stood the waters up like a heap" (Psalm 78:13). And this is different again from the tradition represented in Psalm 105, for example. For the prophets, the exodus tradition becomes an important source for imagining both God's judgment of Israel, as well as its future redemption:

> When you pass through the waters, I am with you;
> and through the rivers, they will not flood you.
> When you walk through fire, you will not be consumed,
> and the flame will not burn you.
> For I am Yhwh your God,
> the holy one of Israel who delivers you. (Isaiah 43:2–3)

In this case, the Isaianic poet—writing during the later period of the Babylonian exile—alludes to the exodus tradition in order to reshape the understanding of God's deliverance and to offer hope. The exodus tradition *also* belongs to the world of the text. In Psalm 66, exodus imagery evokes both the world behind the text and the worlds of the texts themselves, which begins to suggest how these dimensions of context are necessarily overlapping and mutually embedded.

As much as we seek to solidify the poem's historical and literary contexts, though, its language teases our imaginations by opening outward, calling the audience to "go, and see the wonders of God!" (Psalm 66:5). If the speaker is evoking a past memory for the sake of contemporary audiences, what is the function of the past?[4] The psalm is far less interested in describing detailed facts of history and far more interested in fostering a sense of communal experience, such that the event's significance is drawn forward into the present experience of later generations. Where we stand, as readers, is in the world in front of the text. Our concerns shape our perspectives and drive our readings in both conscious and unconscious ways. But we do not stand here alone. Already, the text witnesses to a long legacy of readers. If you are reading a poem in translation, it is through the interpretation of another reader who is looking at the Hebrew and making decisions about how to present it in another language. If you are reading a poem in a critical edition of the Hebrew text, it is through the interpretation of another reader who has prepared the text by making careful judgments about manuscripts. This reader of Hebrew texts is already reading through the interpretive decisions of medieval Jewish scholars who added vowel and cantillation marks to an unpointed text to solidify its meaning. Even earlier than these, the psalm's superscription, "To the leader, a song, a psalm," while spare, is evidence within the text itself of an editor who is supplying interpretive directions about the text's meaning and function. There are generations of readers, in other words, who have handed the text down and given it its current shape and place in the collection. They stand in front of the text, in the worlds of its interpreters.

And since, as we have already seen, not everything can be disclosed by the poem itself, the communities and individuals who read and interpret stand on the far edge of the poem's history, providing yet more contexts in which it lives.[5] Poems are always in search of a reader; readers, we shall see, are necessary to the poem. What does it mean that God "has not let our feet slip"? That God has "tried us as silver is tried"? That "you let people ride over our heads . . . yet you have brought us out to a spacious place" (vv. 9, 10, 12)? Are these references once again to the exodus tradition, as some interpreters think? Or are they allusions to another period of persecution, for example, to the exile, as other interpreters think? The openness of the symbolic register of the poem requires that the reader enter in, supplying much of the meaning that remains undetermined by the text itself. This is the world in front of the text, where readers bring to bear their experiences and judgments, to render sometimes strikingly different interpretations. Readers in African American contexts have often highlighted God's deliverance of the Israelites from slavery as indicative of God's ultimately liberatory vision. This is very different from some contemporary Jewish readings that highlight the story's movement toward the particularity of the Sinai covenant with the Israelites. This is very different again from how readers concerned with contexts of displacement have read the text (First Nations in the Americas, for example, or contemporary Palestine). How readers encounter lines such as these are necessarily shaped by their own personal and communal concerns, both conscious and unconscious.

This chapter will consider some of the poem's broader horizons, where it extends beyond itself, back into the historical context from which it emerges, laterally into adjacent texts, and forward into the future contexts of its readers. These three vectors of context interact in complex ways and are not entirely predictable. So, the goal of exploring a poem's contexts is not to land on the single correct reading. It is to walk with the poem with as much immersive attention as possible, considering how it asks us to orient ourselves toward the world. In what follows, I will focus substantially but not exclusively on prophetic poetry because of the ways that prophecy both exemplifies and muddies these distinctions.

THE WORLDS BEHIND THE TEXT

We begin with a brief sketch. The poetry of the Bible emerged over many centuries—it is possible that almost a millennium passed between the oldest texts, the youngest ones, and the time of their collection. This is a wide swath of historical memory, during which several important transitions were taking place in the ancient world. After the collapse of the great Canaanite city-states of the Bronze Age, there emerged local kingdoms in the Levant, among them the Iron Age kingdoms of Israel and Judah (their emergence is dated to around the tenth–ninth centuries BCE). These communities and their successors would eventually produce the Bible we now have. Under successive, expansive empires of Mesopotamia, these kingdoms fell. The first of these catastrophic events was Assyria's destruction of the northern kingdom of Israel (722 BCE). While the southern kingdom of Judah survived the military incursion of Assyria, it eventually fell to Babylon about 150 years later (586 BCE), which is the second great catastrophe that informs the biblical literature. Babylon deported the people of its conquered territories, and so part of what shapes biblical poetry and its collection is the experience of exile. While it was only a matter of decades before the Persian Empire defeated Babylon and allowed exiles to return to their homelands (538 BCE), the meager population that did return was not able to reinstate their kings or sovereignty. One thing that stands out from this very basic and provisional sketch is that Israel and Judah emerged as connected people and minor nations at a given point in time and space, had a brief span of sovereignty, and were eventually destroyed by incursions from two successive empires. Their poetry, therefore, is keenly attuned to accounts of inception and loss, which it frequently invokes. In Psalm 66, it is Israel's inception that is of keen interest, told in theological terms as a result of divine establishment. With this basic sketch in mind, we will consider some of the ways that different poems engage these complicated worlds behind the text.

In many ways, it is the prophetic poetry that most palpably engages with historical context. The poems tend to be marked as direct address to a historical audience. For this reason, they are sometimes seen as homiletical or rhetorical, though as we shall see such understandings fall short. Their manner of address is quite distinct from the poetry of the psalms, for example, which tends to be speech directed *to* God. The prophetic poems, in contrast, tend to be speech directed *from* God, *to* people (via the prophet; for more on this, see chapter 1). As such, they often identify themselves historically with much greater specificity than other biblical poems. Hosea, for example, opens with this superscription: "The word of Yhwh, which came to Hosea, son of Beeri, in the days of Uzziah, Jotham, Ahaz, and Hezekiah, kings of Judah; and in the days of Jeroboam, son of Joash, king of Israel" (Hosea 1:1). Already, there is a good deal of historical specificity that is highlighted by naming the prophet and the eighth-century kings of Judah and Israel. Some of the poetry collected in Isaiah 1–39, Amos, and Micah also references this period. As collections, though, these prophets are already heavily redacted—they have been edited and rewritten, and so the texts as we have them are already shaped by concerns of other readers in front of the text—though here we can see how this language is slippery. These editors presumably stood as readers "in front of" some earlier version of the text, which was itself the outgrowth of some previous text or tradition. But they are also historical—they stand "behind" the text as we have it. Once again, the contexts of poems are subtle and interwoven.

Hosea's poems address the northern kingdom of Israel (also called "Ephraim," the name of Israel's largest tribe). Beyond the superscription, the poems themselves are saturated with matters of political and historical significance to that ancient context:

> Hear this, O priests!
> Listen, O house of Israel!
> Give ear, O house of the king!
> The judgment is for you;
> for you have been a snare at Mizpah,
> and a net spread out on Tabor,
> and a pit dug deep in Shittim;
> but I will discipline all of them. (Hosea 5:1–2)

The direct address and the specific place-names all locate the text and give it rhetorical directionality. They call our attention to the world behind the text. In these lines, the poet displays a concern about the way that corrupt leadership ("priests," nation, and "king") can have further, corrupting influence on others ("you have been a snare," "a net spread out," "a pit dug deep"). One of the book's governing metaphors is the erotic love between God and people, so a profound concern of these poems is the betrayal of that love. In this pattern of thought, idolatry is conceptualized as adultery. Here, the concrete names of northern towns ("Mizpah," "Tabor," and "Shittim") seem to exemplify sites of cultic infidelity—improper worship—through which Israel is "defiled" (Hosea 5:3). In this sense, prophetic poetry is attentive to what is happening in its current sociopolitical moment. Hosea will go on to say that "Ephraim went to Assyria, / and sent to the great king." Seeking aid or alliance with a threatening foreign enemy, according to the prophet, is another violation of exclusive devotion to God and can only lead to devastation: "But he will not be able to heal you / or to cure your wound" (Hosea 5:13). Bearing such contextual factors in mind, contemporary readers can seek to identify the otherness of the ancient audience and to extend empathy for their situation and concerns.

ALLUSION

While the poetry of Hosea is engaged in the world behind the text, it is also a body of work that is deeply allusive, aware of other traditions, and speaking in a way that assumes the audience is also aware of these traditions. These poems speak of previous prophets (6:5) and of a "covenant" that has been violated (6:7). They show an awareness of some of the founding stories of Israel, for example Jacob's establishment of a sanctuary at Bethel and wrestling with God at Penuel, stories found now in the book of Genesis (Hosea 12:3–4). They also are aware of traditions about Moses leading the Israelites out of bondage and of their wandering in the wilderness, stories found now in the books of Exodus and Numbers (Hosea 9:10, 12:13). These can usefully be thought of as allusions, echoes of other traditions that are one dimension of the world of the text. The examples from Hosea are somewhat fuzzy, insofar as they gesture to traditions by name but do not directly quote them. Hosea begins to suggest, though, that the texts of the Bible are already in relationship to other texts—they refer to one another and develop their own later insights by reworking earlier ones.

Here is another example from the poetry collections of Isaiah. This text likely comes from the eighth century BCE and includes a fantastic vision of the scale of the world's future peace (often referred to as "the peaceable kingdom"):

The wolf will dwell with the lamb,
and the leopard will lie down with the goat;

> the calf and the lion and the fatted calf together,
> and a little child will lead them.
> The cow and bear will graze,
> together their young will lie down,
> and the lion will eat straw like the ox.
> The nursing child will play over the hole of the adder,
> and over the viper's den
> the weaned child will put his hand.
> They will not harm or destroy on all my holy mountain,
> for the earth will be full of the knowledge of Yhwh
> as the waters cover the sea. (Isaiah 11:6–9)

For the post-exilic poet, writing some centuries later, the same words continue to ring true, and they are reapplied to a new context in a gesture that seems to intentionally evoke the previous text and to extend its meaning to new circumstances:

> The wolf and the lamb will graze as one,
> and the lion will eat straw like the ox,
> and the serpent will have dust for food.
> They will not harm and or destroy on all my holy mountain,
> says Yhwh. (Isaiah 65:25)

The reiteration of these specific images for a fifth-century BCE context renews the eschatological imagination for a new era, and it offers an expansive vision of international peace during a time when—perhaps for the first time in centuries—such a thing might have seemed tantalizingly within reach.

There is a certain unpredictability to an allusion, since it relies on the audience's (variable) knowledge and memory, and on the audience's (variable) ability to put the two texts into a meaningful relationship. We can see from these examples that an allusion is not mere repetition; rather, it is a trope, a figurative device that plays with the gap between text and meaning. Allusions will operate unpredictably because they require the knowledge and imaginative engagement of the reader. Allusions ask that earlier texts be read in new contexts, for which they will take on new shapes, forms, and meanings.[6] This can be seen writ large among the texts of the New Testament, which are constantly taking up texts from the Hebrew Bible as they reconstrue earlier texts in light of their new (Christian) interpretive aims. Consider, for example, the placement of Psalm 22 in the Book of Common Prayer's Daily Office on Good Friday, a day that liturgically indexes the crucifixion of Jesus. This placement acknowledges that two of the Gospel accounts describe Jesus uttering the words "My God, my God, why have you forsaken me?" the opening lines of Psalm 22, from the cross (Matthew 27:46; Mark 15:34). This placement by Christian readers actively encourages a Christological interpretation of the psalm—a move that is, of course, rejected by Jewish and non-Christian readers. But the tendency to read the Psalms forward as prophecy is familiar to both Jews and Christians: during the Second Temple period (around the time of Jesus), there is evidence that many readers—both Jews and Christians—understood the entire book of Psalms as prophecy.[7] For first-century audiences, these poems were directed toward the future. As the example of Psalm 22 suggests, the relationships between texts are already bound up with the world in front of the text, which is to say, they are always shaped by the concerns of their readers.

PROPHETIC POETRY'S REFUSALS

So far, we have seen ways that the three "worlds" of the text are intertwined. This is acutely the case for the prophetic poems, which are more directly related to historical contexts and are consistently reappropriated by later readers to address new contexts. But I want to pause for a brief caveat: there are competing tensions about context in many prophetic poems. On the one hand, the prophets are keenly interested in exposing sin and in predicting punishment—so, they are tuned to a historical audience. On the other hand, the prophets regularly make recourse to a language that is non-disclosive, metaphorical, and oblique. There is much of biblical prophecy that is surprisingly reticent to directly name or describe people and events in any detail. Prophetic poems trouble the reader with unsettling imagery, but they also can tend to resist straightforward interpretation. Here is an example, from a bit further along in Hosea, where the poet speaks of Ephraim:

> All of them adulterers
> are like an oven that burns,
> whose baker does not need to stoke the fire
> from the kneading of the dough until it is leavened.
> On the day of our king our leaders are sickened
> with the heat of wine.
> He stretched out his hand to the scoffers.
> For they are kindled like an oven,
> their heart burns within them:
> All night their baker slumbers;
> in the morning it blazes like a flaming fire.
> All of them are hot as an oven,
> and they devour their rulers.
> All their kings have fallen;
> none of them calls upon me. (Hosea 7:4–7)

What is so striking here is the imagery, which is evocative and outsize. Israel's "adultery" burns, like an oven so hot it does not need to be tended, raging with exceptional heat. This is underscored by a repetitive fixation on the oven: Israel is an "oven," that "burns," so hot it need not be "stoked" (v. 4); their rulers "become hot" (v. 5); they are "kindled like an oven," their heart "burns," and their anger "burns like a flaming fire" (v. 6); they are "hot as an oven," that consumes (v. 7). The poetry here lifts off from the specific historical context as it creates a surreal, metaphorical world centering on an uncanny, dangerous oven. In Hosea's eroticized thought-world, what "burns" suggests lust for what is not-God.

As it develops this metaphor of the oven, though, the poem resists attempts to fully explain it. Why, for example, are the leaders "sickened with the heat of wine" (v. 5)? What does wine have to do with an oven? The poem relates the two with the shared image of "heat," but now layered over the previous metaphor is a sense of the dizzying stupor of drunkenness, which leads to "devouring" rulers (v. 7). Is it the fire that devours? Or the drunken leaders? If there is an actual historical event in view here, it recedes behind a vibrant bricolage of arresting images. They puzzle the reader, as they might have also puzzled the original audience. For the poet, the images themselves are profoundly important—otherwise, why employ them at all?

To press this point further, in the passage that follows, Ephraim is now not an oven, but a cake:

> Ephraim mixes himself with the peoples;
> Ephraim is a cake not turned.
> Foreigners devour his strength,
> but he does not know it.
> Gray hairs are sprinkled upon him,
> but he does not know it. (Hosea 7:8–9)

Now Ephraim is not doing the devouring but is being devoured by foreigners. The refrain here "but he does not know it" (twice in v. 9) signals the confusion the poem imputes to Ephraim. But this confusion is not only imputed—it is also created by the experience of the poem, whose quickly shifting metaphors raise questions. This is rhetorically effective insofar as it destabilizes the audience (assuming that Israelites would have been the audience and not the subject only), but it also refuses a great deal. There is much that the poem simply will not tell us. Like Ephraim, we, too "do not know it." Instead, we are asked to inhabit the bizarre, unmoored imagination of the poem, which stretches beyond its historical context to make us imagine what motivates disloyalty to God, and what conditions unfaithfulness can create on a grand scale.

We assume too much when we assume that an "original audience" could easily perceive the poem's meaning, and that we
have simply lost access to it through time and history. Just as some
contemporary art (including poetry) tends toward the obscure, so
too does some ancient art. The ending of the book underscores
this point:

> Whoever is wise, let him understand these things.
> Whoever has understanding, let him know them.
> For the ways of the Lord are upright
> and the righteous walk in them,
> but sinners will stumble over them. (Hosea 14:9)

This implies that the meaning is not self-evident but must be discerned by a reader "wise" and "understanding" enough to "know."
The lines suggest a later reader already concerned with the difficulty
of interpreting these poems which, the writer seems to acknowledge, are as likely as not to cause someone to "stumble over them."
These lines are also an invitation, gesturing forward to latecomers
who will encounter the prophetic texts at a far remove from where
they may have been first delivered. In this way, the text displays a
self-consciousness about the future-directedness of poetry that is
written down. These lines assume a stance of complicity: they encourage later audiences to consider the poems carefully as objects
of knowledge, admitting that such a task might be difficult. Indeed,
they even ascribe to the poems a certain amount of power to reject
the inquiry of some, to whom they will remain closed off.

Isaiah of Jerusalem (this is how I will refer to the poet(s) of
those texts in Isaiah 1–39) makes this recalcitrant dimension of the
prophetic poetry explicit. He describes the task of prophesying in
the following way:

> And he (God) said: "Go and say to this people:
> 'Listen closely, but do not understand;
> look intently, but do not perceive.'

Dull this people's heart,
and stop their ears,
and seal their eyes—
Lest they see with their eyes,
and hear with their ears,
and perceive with their minds,
and turn and be healed." (Isaiah 6:9–10)

The role of the prophetic poet, as it is imagined here, is not to expose sin through a rhetoric that is transparent. Instead, it is part
of the task of the poem to create difficulty that will prevent understanding (which, in this case, will by extension prevent forgiveness). This text shows an awareness that at least some of the
prophetic poetry is not intended to be rhetorically directed and
effectively communicative. While scholars often describe this passage as evidence of the people's "harsh rejection of (Isaiah's) message,"[8] no actual rejection of any kind is described. Instead, this
part of the poem centers on the eyes and ears of the people. Its
main technique is simple repetition (the verbs "to hear" and "to
see" are each repeated three times; "ears" and "eyes" and "heart" are
each repeated twice; "perceive" is repeated twice). It is *perception*—
not rejection—that offers itself as an object of consideration. For
Isaiah, there is an intentional will to stymie perception. It's not that
they will "reject," according to Isaiah, but that they will not "understand" or "know."

Contemporary readers might note that this is not an uncommon experience in reading poems—to feel they are difficult,
or opaque, and that reading or hearing them is not enough to access their meaning. In Biblical Hebrew, as today, language permits
various levels of disclosure. The highly wrought, densely crafted
quality of some biblical poems can make their meanings difficult to unravel. For our purposes here, these observations suggest
that while the prophetic poets are deeply rooted in their historical
contexts, not everything they write can be directly correlated to
those contexts. This is not only a function of our own ignorance

and distance in time and place (though it is partly that), it is also a function of poetic style. If the only goal of the prophetic poetry were to make God's will known to the people, then a straightforward declarative style would presumably be more effective. That the prophets write poetry—sometimes deeply obscure poetry— suggests that their purposes are more complex. Poems can hover at this point of potentiality, where they verge toward but ultimately resist decisive meaning.[9] This potentiality makes them profoundly open to the interests of later interpreters. This text of Isaiah, for example, both addresses and resists its eighth-century BCE context, as I have suggested. For early Christian interpreters, this pluripotentiality of the prophets allowed them to read this particular text forward through the centuries to the life of Jesus of Nazareth, including these very lines from Isaiah 6.[10] Situating texts in their contexts as much as possible is appropriate and useful because it resists subsuming or denying the history of the texts and their cultural specificity. (For many Christian readers, denying Isaiah's work as a Judahite in Jerusalem was part and parcel of a hostile anti-Jewish theological program, and should be rigorously critiqued.)[11] Yet, textual indeterminacy is also part of what has given these poems profound power for later communities. Presumably, readers after us will find in them yet more potential meanings. To acknowledge poetry's openness requires a certain existential humility on the part of readers: we are neither these poems' first readers nor their last.

THE POETRY OF EXILE

The poems discussed so far were mostly situated in eighth-century BCE contexts. But probably the single most important event in the world behind the text for understanding the collections of biblical poetry is the destruction of Jerusalem by Babylon a century and half later, in 586 BCE. This destruction, and the subsequent exile of many of its citizens, is a collective trauma that exercised a powerful influence on its literature. Many texts bear witness to the event itself, and it seems to be the case that most of the texts of the Bible as we now have them were compiled and edited under the conditions of this catastrophe.[12] The poems of Lamentations, which have been discussed a bit in chapter 3, are a central witness to this devastation. In this poetry, the figure of personified Jerusalem gives voice to her suffering:

> See, O Yhwh, that I am distraught.
> My stomach churns;
> my heart within me turns
> because I have been very rebellious.
> Outside, the sword consumes;
> inside, it is like death. (Lamentations 1:20)

These poems speak to the experience of siege warfare. The siege of Jerusalem lasted almost two years. The poems describe the appalling conditions of sickness, starvation, and terror within a walled city under siege. As the last couplet of Lamentations 1:20 notes, the "sword" is outside, and inside "it is like death." The totality of suffering during war, from which there is no refuge, is the consuming focus of this poetry. It calls attention to the horrific costs of war.

The prophetic poetry of both Ezekiel and Jeremiah is also situated during the destruction of Jerusalem and the exile. Ezekiel's poetry, written from the perspective of the people in exile, is particularly caustic and deranged. These poems evoke a world turned upside down. By situating the poetry in this world behind the text, we can better access the intellectual work of Ezekiel's art, which attempts to provide new strategies of cultural survival after the trauma of exile. Ezekiel's work is a mix of poetry and prose; the two are often interwoven in highly imagistic poetic prose and prose-y poetry. The first long poem is an anticipation of destruction; the word "the end!" (*qets*) is repeated several times (Ezekiel 7:2, 3, 6), but the emphasis is not on the armies of Babylon, but on the hand of God: "I will judge you according to your ways, / I will repay you for all your abominations" (Ezekiel 7:3). In this way, the divine voice recontextualizes social and political disruption as the work of Israel's own God. While this has the ring of victim blaming, it is doing theological work insofar as it does not evade immanent disaster but faces it headlong, maintaining a sense of control in the face of disaster.[13]

Later in the collection, Ezekiel offers a vision of both judgment and restoration. Ezekiel 19 calls for a "lamentation" for the princes of Israel. Here, the poem envisions a powerful mother lion who raised a cub that "learned to catch prey; / he devoured humans" (Ezekiel 19:3). He eventually was "caught in (the hunter's) pit; / and they brought him with hooks to the land of Egypt" (Ezekiel 19:4). Another "cub" also becomes powerful. He, too, "learned to catch prey; / he devoured humans" (Ezekiel 19:6). He was hunted by "nations," who

> spread their net over him;
> he was caught in their pit.
> With hooks they put him in a cage,
> and brought him to the king of Babylon . . . (Ezekiel 19:8–9)

Here, multiple contexts seem to be in play. First, the poem draws on a tradition in the visual arts of the ancient Near East, in which rulers—kings—are depicted as lions. Here, that imagery is deployed in a way that seems to allude specifically to this royal ideology of power. The specific references to the lion being "taken to Babylon" are suggestive: Do we imagine that the poem is talking about particular Judahite kings? From 2 Kings 23:31–34, we learn of Jehoahaz, the son of the Queen Mother Hamutal and Josiah, who was captured by Pharaoh Neco and taken to Egypt. Both the later kings Jehoiakin and Zedekiah were eventually exiled to Babylon; does the poem have one of those kings in mind? We run into trouble trying to tease out the exact motivating historical context here, and the expansiveness of the imagery itself suggests that such contexts are inexact. After all, the poem describes the "cubs" as having one "mother," which lifts the poem into the realm of metaphor. Is the "mother" a person at all? Or the nation of Judah? The latter reading is made more compelling by the latter half of the "lamentation," which describes the mother "like a vine in a vineyard" (Ezekiel 19:10). As discussed earlier (see chapter 4), the vineyard is a potent image in biblical literature for the nation of Israel. The poem draws on these contexts as its imagery mourns disestablishment:

> Now she is transplanted in the wilderness,
> in a dry and thirsty land . . .
> She has no strong stem,
> no scepter for ruling. (Ezekiel 19:13–14, selections)

Trauma prompts new creative work. The poetry of Ezekiel wrestles with the problem of theodicy—why does God allow for the suffering of God's own people? One answer that the poetry offers is assigning responsibility—as Ezekiel 7 does, by suggesting that Israel is culpable and is being punished for its sins. Another answer is suggested by Ezekiel 19, which does not assign blame for the predicament of exile. Instead, it offers a meditation on the loss of sovereignty, using traditional symbols to give a visual language to the grief of loss.

Of course, not all poetry of the exile is as bracing as Ezekiel's. The poetry of Isaiah 40–55 ("Deutero-Isaiah" or "Second Isaiah") includes some of the most beloved poetry of the Bible:

> Comfort, oh comfort my people,
> says your God.
> Speak to the heart of Jerusalem,
> and cry to her
> that she has fulfilled her service,
> that her penalty is pardoned,
> that she has received from Yhwh's hand
> double for all her sins. (Isaiah 40:1–2)

This text engages the world behind the text—it too speaks of exile, but in a new moment of political hope when Cyrus of Persia (ca. 600–530 BCE) had decreed that peoples exiled under Babylon might return to their homelands.[14] The text reconfigures exile through engagement with the world of the text, by alluding perhaps directly to the poetry of Lamentations (the city "has no comforter," Lamentations 1:2) and by recasting the exodus tradition in order to imagine the "new thing" that God is bringing about. The exodus memory of liberation provides the topos of this new liberation, return from exile:

> Thus says the Lord,
> who makes a way in the sea,
> a path in the mighty waters,
> who brings out chariot and horse,
> army and warrior . . .
> Do not remember the former things,
> or consider the things of old.
> I am about to do a new thing;
> now it springs forth; do you not perceive it?
> I will make a way in the wilderness,
> rivers in the desert. (Isaiah 43:16–19)

As can be seen in both Ezekiel and the poetry of Second Isaiah, the catastrophe of 586 BCE prompted both a reassessment of old texts and traditions as well as literary innovation. Developing our sense of the worlds poems come from is one way of understanding the work they are accomplishing as art. This allows us, too, a measure for interpretations—while there are always multiple possible ways of looking at a text, this need not imply that all interpretations are necessarily equal.[15] It is possible and necessary to adjudicate among different readings, and contexts can provide some parameters (albeit not ultimate ones) for doing so.

PSALM 137: A READING

The catastrophe of 586 BCE also gives us Psalm 137, a haunting poem that is famous for its brutal final lines:

> O Daughter Babylon, you devastator!
> Happy is the one who pays you back
> what you have done to us.
> Happy is the one who seizes and shatters
> your little ones on the rock. (Psalm 137: 8–9)

This is a rare psalm that speaks so directly about the world behind the text. But in this reading, I begin with recent readers in the world in front of the text. Students encountering Psalm 137's cry of rage have sometimes told me that such texts are the reason they reject the Bible—because it of its ancient, savage violence. Certainly, as I will show, interpreters over the centuries have also rejected this psalm in various ways, often by spiritualizing it or by refusing to read it altogether. But over and over through its interpretive history, Psalm 137 has also been a resource for communities facing state-sponsored violence, whether that state is ancient Babylon, or Rome, or modern Germany, or the United States of America.

This book was completed in the weeks following the guilty verdict in the case of the former Minneapolis police officer who murdered George Floyd, Jr. on May 25, 2020. The year has been marked both by the prolonged communal impacts of COVID-19 and by sweeping protests against police brutality, racial violence, and discrimination. It is impossible for me to read Psalm 137 under these grave and electrifying circumstances without considering the resemblances between these outraged cries for justice, set so far apart in time. It is instructive to note how Black thinkers have appealed to the language of the psalms and the particular language of Psalm 137 to memorialize and protest suffering. Rodney Sadler writes: "The Psalter provided a vocabulary for early African and African American authors to exclaim their greatest joys and mourn their bitterest disappointments, a script that reflected their own struggles with the world and with God."[16] Psalm 137 becomes a script of this sort in the work of Frederick Douglass, in his Address at the Graves of the Unknown Dead at Arlington (1871),[17] and in W. E. B. Du Bois's "A Litany of Atlanta," protesting the massacre of African Americans by an armed White mob in 1906.[18] Joining these voices, a recent poem by Reginald Dwayne Betts entitled "When I Think of Tamir Rice While Driving" meditates on parenting Black sons in a world where a Tamir Rice, a twelve-year-old Black boy carrying a toy gun, was killed by a White police officer. Central to the poem is the contrast between the speaker's young boys, playing innocently in the backseat of his car, and the death of Tamir Rice, which plays on a loop in the speaker's memory. The scene is punctuated with this line: "My tongue cleaves to the roof / of my mouth, my right hand has forgotten."[19] This is a reference to two verses of Psalm 137, which I quote here in the King James Version, since Betts's language most closely echoes this translation:

> If I forget thee, O Jerusalem, let my right hand forget her cunning.
> If I do not remember thee, let my tongue cleave to the roof of my mouth;
> If I prefer not Jerusalem above my chief joy. (Psalm 137:5–6)

How do these gestures to an ancient psalm signify? Read in light of protests against entrenched racial violence, we might see how Psalm 137 demands that its readers consider carefully the place of rage, because the language of violence is the language of the person who has not been heard. I echo here the words of Martin Luther King, Jr., speaking of race riots in the 1960s: " . . . a riot is the language of the unheard. And what is it America has failed to hear? It has failed to hear that the plight of the Negro poor has worsened over the last few years."[20] One of the powerful potentials of Psalm 137 is to offer a voice to those in fear of or victimized by state-sponsored violence.

Slowly working our way through the poem, we will see how the various worlds of the text can illuminate the complex realities of trauma and rage, both in the ancient world and today.

Psalm 137 is unique among the psalms in its historical concreteness. It locates itself geographically, in Babylon, and temporally, during the exile in the aftermath of the disaster of 586 BCE. In the first section of the poem, nearly every line contains a reference to place:

> By (ʿal) the rivers of Babylon
> there we sat down and wept
> when we remembered Zion.
> Upon (ʿal) the willows there
> we hung our harps.
> For there they asked us:
> our captors (asked us) for words of a song;
> our tormentors (asked us) for mirth:
> "Sing for us a song of Zion!"
> How could we sing a song of Yhwh
> on (ʿal) foreign soil? (Psalm 137:1–4)

"Thereness" is the prompting problem of the poem, which is revealed in the first line and reiterated in almost every line of the next ten. Over and over the speaker specifies geographical location. The three lines that begin with ʿal (on, upon) locate the speaker. We are in "Babylon," a place of rivers and willows, a strange and foreign place. It is, the poem insists, not "here" but "there." But Zion (Jerusalem) is not "here" either; it is only remembered, an occasion for mourning. These ʿal lines are coupled with descriptions of resignation: "there we sat down and wept," "we hung our harps," "how could we sing a song of Yhwh on foreign soil?" The sense of dislocation is held alongside an insistence on communal identity. Here, the collective voice "we," "our" echoes throughout. This is even more apparent in Hebrew, where the first-person plural suffix -nu refers eight times in these four verses to the communal speaker.

This creates a kind of music, a soft insistence on the shared experience of loss. Because the poem refers to the "day of Jerusalem" on which the city was stripped to its foundations, and yet refers to Babylon as if it is still in power, it may have been composed between 586 BCE and 539 BCE (when Babylon was taken over by Persia), though this is speculative. Regardless of exactly when it was written, the psalm speaks about a particular experience of catastrophic loss—a particular place and a particular time in the world behind the text.

But even its early readers found in Psalm 137's specific evocation of historical loss a vocabulary for articulating other experiences of victimization. This is connected to the theological treatment of the psalms as prophecy. Some early Greek translations include a superscription reading "to David," or "a psalm of David through Jeremiah." These ascribe the psalm to a much earlier time and recast it not as a reflection on a historical event, but as a prophetic expectation of a future one. This projection about future suffering is all the more explicit in later linkages of this psalm not to the destruction of the First Temple in Jerusalem in 586 BCE, but to the destruction of the Second Temple in Jerusalem by Rome in 70 CE. A Talmudic text explains the text's future orientation in this way:

> Said R. Yehuda: Rab said: (This psalm) proves that God showed to David the destruction of the First Temple and the destruction of the Second. The First Temple as it is said, "by the rivers of Babylon," the Second Temple as it is said, "Call to account, O Lord, the Edomites for the Day of Jerusalem."[21]

Instead of understanding the reference to the "Edomites" in verse 7 as a reference to the nation who aided Babylon's destruction of Jerusalem in the sixth century BCE, the term was taken to refer to Rome, in light of its common later usage in Jewish texts. In this way, early interpretations of the text understood its historical context in broadening terms—expanding its horizons backward into the past *and* forward into the future. These readers saw in the text a potential to speak to their current experiences of state-sponsored violence. This future orientation persists: in a 2010 opera by Robert Saxton, *The Wandering Jew*, Psalm 137 is sung by the chorus in a Nazi death camp.[22] "Babylon" becomes an expansive trope for experiences of barbarism and collective trauma, and the psalm as a whole fittingly memorializes new atrocities and communal suffering.

As the poem goes on, it is rich with layers of tragic irony—their captors have asked them to sing: "Sing for us a song of Zion!" (Psalm 137:3). But this is an impossibility. The poem emphasizes the experience of otherness: it is not that the songs are forgotten, but that they cannot be sung "on foreign soil." Here, there is a subtle glance to the literary world of the text. Among the psalms are a small collection of hymns sometimes called "Zion Songs" that celebrate Yhwh's sanctuary and affirm Zion's unassailability: "Great is Yhwh and much acclaimed / in the city of our God, / his holy mountain!" (Psalm 48:1); "God is in the midst (of the city); it will not be moved" (Psalm 46:5).[23] After the assault and defeat of Jerusalem, such poems no doubt seemed incoherent, and Psalm 137 bitterly refuses them.[24] Seeing Psalm 137 in this literary context helps bring into relief two major theological problems confronted by those in exile. First, Jerusalem, understood to be founded by God and unassailable, had been destroyed. Second, the kingship of an heir of David, understood to be an eternal guarantee, was no longer in existence. The resulting psychological and spiritual discord of these losses is part of the energy that generates Psalm 137. How, in light of these disruptions, could it be possible to "sing a song of Yhwh on foreign soil"? The text rejects this dimension of its world, offering instead a vivid image of cultural impossibility: instruments hang in the willow trees, where they will not be played (Psalm 137:2).

The question of the role of art will continue to vex the poem:

If I forget you, O Jerusalem,
let my right hand forget.

> Let my tongue cling to my palate
> if I do not remember,
> if I do not place Jerusalem
> above my highest joy. (Psalm 137:5–6)

The right hand and the tongue represent implements of art. The right hand is often associated with agency or power in biblical texts, but it is also quintessentially the hand used for writing, and the tongue is associated with speech and song.[25] The two together suggest the poet's ability: to write, and to speak or sing. It may be the case that Psalm 137 originates from a temple musician, for whom singing and playing instruments would have been indispensable to their vocation.[26] But even though we cannot be confident of this more specific reconstruction of the world behind the text, we can note the poem's reflection on the creative act: the hand and tongue are invoked in a self-curse that vows to remember the past. These are the lines used by Betts in writing about Tamir Rice, in which he aligns himself with the ancient and vital task of the poet who witnesses atrocity, the task of remembrance. In the psalm, remembrance moves in two diverging directions. On the one hand, the poem insists that the old songs can no longer be sung. On the other hand, Psalm 137 itself is a new song with a vow never to forget. There is a strained relationship between old and new—between memory and innovation—brought about by the trauma of destruction and forced migration. It would seem like the old songs are exactly what will preserve the memory of what has been lost. But the poem instead insists on the creation of new texts as a pathway for memory.

Then the voicing shifts again, and the speaker turns to directly address the deity:

> Remember, O Yhwh, against the Edomites
> on the day of Jerusalem,
> how they said, "Tear it down! Tear it down
> to its foundations!" (Psalm 137:7)

Instead of focusing on human memory, the poem cries out for divine solidarity with human suffering. The address will shift once more in the final lines, to speak to Babylon itself:

> O Daughter Babylon, you devastator!
> Happy is the one who pays you back
> what you have done to us.
> Happy is the one who seizes and shatters
> your little ones on the rock. (Psalm 137: 8–9)

The force of the final line is so harrowing that it almost eclipses the powerful rhetorical move here: the address to Babylon. The great conceit of these lines is that the speaker can speak directly to the nation that destroyed them. In the lived experience of victims of such acts of political domination, there is no such opportunity. It is a great imaginative act that takes place here, an act that seeks to reclaim a sense of agency and identity in a hopeless situation. This text enables victims (specifically the ancient exiles and also later audiences) to imagine what they might say if they had an audience with their assailants. This is an opportunity denied to most victims of all kinds—political and personal. What the victim demands is justice. The poem uses technical language ("to pay back," *yeshallem*, in the piel stem) for repayment in kind. It asks for perpetrators of war to suffer what they themselves have inflicted. Other texts use the disturbing language of the destruction of little ones as a way of conveying the horrors of war, as for example the prophetic poetry of Hosea: "Therefore the mayhem will rise against your people, / and all your fortresses will be destroyed, / as Shalman destroyed Beth-arbel on a day of battle / when mothers were dashed in pieces with their children" (Hosea 10:14).[27] The dashing to pieces of innocent women and children is an image that, when it is used in biblical texts, is used by sufferers to make vivid their suffering. It is not the language of victors in celebration, it is the language of victims in despair. The plea for retributive justice here in Psalm 137 must be understood in this literary context. It calls to mind first and foremost the injustice that the community has suffered in the violent indifference of war. It imagines having an audience with the powerful nation who has devastated them, giving voice to those who have endured destruction and exile. This is where the imagination of repayment in kind emerges: devastation of war for the devastation of war.

What is imagined here, though, is deeply troubling. So troubling, in fact, that it has prompted many interpreters to deny or ameliorate it. This is perhaps most evident in the prominent trend in Christian interpretation to spiritualize the psalm. Jerome, the fourth-century church leader, opens his commentary with a brief preface explaining that Psalm 137 should be understood in three dimensions: First, as addressing the exile of the Jews in Babylon; second, as addressing the practice of expelling sinners from the Christian church; and third, as a psalm about "the superior exile, by which a sometimes noble company is led forth into the vale of tears."[28] By this "superior exile," Jerome pushes the reader to see themselves in a kind of spiritual "Babylon" of a sinful world, in exile from their true, heavenly home. This is perhaps most famously and influentially rendered by Augustine, whose spiritualized reading interprets the final verses as an appropriate way of harshly circumscribing one's sins:

> Who are these little ones in Babylon? Evil desires newly come to birth. Some people have to fight against inveterate desires, but you can do better than that. When an evil desire is born, before your bad habits reinforce it, while it is still in its infancy and has not fortified itself by alliance with depraved custom, dash it to pieces. It is only a baby still. But make sure it does not survive your violent treatment: dash it on the rock. *And the rock is Christ* (1 Cor. 10:4).[29]

While Augustine does not express an active discomfort with the violence of these verses, the spiritualized reading suggests that he was reading around a challenging dimension of the text at hand. In many contemporary Christian and Jewish liturgical contexts (including hymns, lectionary readings, and other settings for public use) the final verses of this psalm are simply omitted. This, too, suggests an interpretive discomfort with the cry for violence.[30] These interpreters, by denying the poem's ending, or by spiritualizing it, resist the extremity of its outcry against injustice.

In Du Bois's "A Litany of Atlanta," he evokes the same kind of rage that we hear at the end of Psalm 137, pleading with God for justice:

> Doth not this justice of hell stink in Thy nostrils, O God? How long shall the mounting flood of innocent blood roar in Thine ears and pound in our hearts for vengeance? Pile the pale frenzy of blood-crazed brutes who do such deeds high on Thine altar, Jehovah Jireh, and burn it in hell forever and forever!
>
> *Forgive us, good Lord; we know not what we say!*

In the refrains throughout the poem—italicized—is a voice in dialogue with the rest of the prayer. It is a voice that acknowledges how terrifying the lust for violence is, even as the poem articulates its necessity. Betts's contemporary poem on the death of Tamir Rice includes an analogous self-examination of the disturbing desire to see another human being die: "What if all I had stomach for was blood?" These are not the same as the interpretive traditions of spiritualizing Psalm 137, but they share with that tradition the sense of trepidation about how deep the outrage of the victimized can run. The poems themselves are a site where these troubling dynamics are negotiated and memorialized.

New contexts call for cultural renewal: the re-evaluation of former traditions, and the creation of new ones. Psalm 137 emblemizes this process, as it rejects the former songs of Zion and insists on a renewal of art. It embodies a radical departure from other psalms. It does not follow any known forms: it is not a hymn, or a lament, or an acrostic. Its innovation is born from the demands of historical memory, and the need to honor and to re-enact the rituals of place: "Let my tongue cling to my palate / if I do not remember, / if I do not place Jerusalem / above my highest joy" (Psalm 137:6). Bellinger writes that "the poetic effect is that this anti-Zion song insures the future of Zion songs by way of its central and pervasive theme of memory. The text presents a paradox. Singing songs of Zion is impossible, but this powerful text is anything but silent."[31] The psalm commemorates the difficulty of commemoration. It remembers the suffering of victims by exploring one particular facet of the dilemma faced by a community that has experienced trauma: it examines the vital role of art and liturgy in cultural survival. When former works of cultural memory cannot effectively speak to experiences of dislocation, deep personal and communal loss, and the threat of annihilation, new poems need to be written.

Contemporary poet and critic James Longenbach writes of the work of reading poetry: "The language will give us pleasure because it gives us work to do, work that can never be completed no matter how fully explained the poem might be."[32] Part of the pleasure of reading is that it gives us work to do, the work of making texts meaningful, the work of making our lives meaningful. This work cannot be completed but always offers more space to new readers and new readings. There can also be pain in reading a poem. Sometimes, as perhaps in the case of Psalm 137, the pain outweighs the pleasure. Perhaps for some, the pain itself might be a kind of incandescent beauty, terrible and necessary in moments of particular anguish. The work of reading is not necessarily easy, but is myriad, demanding, and morally complex. It requires patient consideration of the poem in its diverging contexts, and the extension of empathy to readers and writers of the past. If we take the sometimes outrageous and often obscure poetry of the prophets as our guide, we will have to come to terms with our own ignorance, and perhaps make peace with our frustration when sense does not easily yield itself to us. The work requires deliberation. Decisions will have to be made. For some readers and some communities, the decision will be not to read Psalm 137, or not all of it, in particular contexts. But to make such a decision, we must first do the work of reading, which calls us out of ourselves into other worlds. The work of the poem calls us not only to historical pasts we have not known before but also into a fuller experience of the present moment, with its changing obligations and ethical urgency. Perhaps, if we let it, the poem might also call us to better futures.

Conclusion

Giving Poetry Life

IN THESE CHAPTERS, I HAVE POINTED to some of the formal dimensions of biblical poems as a credible way of keeping the artwork in the center of the conversation. Voices, lines, forms, and figures are some of the most tangible dimensions of poems, shaping the poem and the reader's or hearer's experience of the poem. Developing an awareness of these dimensions is part of the journey toward better and richer readings. In my final chapter on contexts, I took a broader look at the way that poems are situated, both in the inscrutable past (in which they were composed and read) and in the also inscrutable present (where we are, as readers). To say that readers are also historical is to acknowledge that unless we read or recite or otherwise engage the poem now, it remains only marks on a page. Ultimately, reading is the work that gives poetry life.

To some readers, talking about formal features might feel a bit fusty. The discourse about poetry in the twentieth-century Anglo-American tradition has been deeply shaped by formalism (what is often referred to as "New Criticism"), a tradition marked by the practices of close reading, which tend to assume that the poem is a closed object that contains its meaning in an intricate interrelationship of its parts.[1] Readings in this vein tend to suppress interest in historical dimensions (the author, the social, political, and historical context, etc.) as well as the affective dimensions of readerly experience. This kind of approach to biblical poetry can be seen, for example, in Robert Alter's influential *The Art of Biblical Poetry*.[2] Such

An Invitation to Biblical Poetry. Elaine T. James, Oxford University Press. © Oxford University Press 2022.
DOI: 10.1093/oso/9780190664923.003.0007

approaches have come under considerable suspicion, and for good reason—they can tend to skirt the political and historical dimensions of texts and even deny or suppress the ideologically loaded and messy work of interpretation. Even more structuralist tendencies can be seen in approaches to biblical poems that prefer syllable counting and linguistic analysis, which tend to treat poems as research sites for other kinds of knowledge, not as ends in themselves.

I have attempted to chart a slightly different path. These chapters acknowledge and engage various ways in which poems remain distinctly open—to the cultures that shaped their production, to the political and theological interests that drive their inquiry, and to the readers who confront them. This approach owes a significant debt to the thinking of a variety of philosophers, and poststructuralist and feminist theorists, which I have noted here and there in my footnotes for the interested reader. Throughout the analyses, the reader will note that multiple hermeneutical stances toward the text are invited. It is possible to read biblical poetry with an aim to critically expose and deconstruct its ideologies. It is always equally possible to accept any given poem's terms or to reject them. Most readings for most readers will probably require some mix of acceptance and resistance. In this approach, I have not assumed that there is a single correct stance toward any text nor a single correct reading (though there will always be readings that are more and less compelling). As I believe the poets are free in their acts of creating, so too are readers in their acts of re-creating.

As I have already suggested in the introduction, there is nothing that can replace the act of reading—and I mean "reading" in the broadest possible sense, which includes actually reading with our eyes (whether quietly or out loud), or otherwise hearing, singing, reciting, or experiencing poems. These are embodied, sense experiences with poems at their center. So, throughout this book I have kept individual poems in focus in order to show how they can unfold in meaningful ways and repay careful attention. I have hoped to show that the aesthetic can be a place of profound intellectual engagement. Poems understood in this way are not merely a pleasant way to pass the time (though they can also be that), nor are they merely a way to encode particular values (though they can also do that). Instead, to think of the aesthetic in these terms is to see that the work artists do in composition is inextricable from the work that audiences do in perception. We engage poems and activate them in meaningful ways as we seek to make sense of ourselves and our lives and our experiences. We are able to do this insofar as we assume that the ancient poets were composing and reciting and preserving poetry to make sense of themselves and their lives and their experiences, however different those lives and experiences were from our own.

John Dewey describes this process as an experience of active engagement. To read a poem is not merely to uncover a meaning that already exists. Instead,

> a new poem is created by everyone who reads poetically—not that its *raw* material is original for, after all, we live in the same old world, but that every individual brings with him, when he exercises his individuality, a way of seeing and feeling that in its interaction with old material creates something new, something previously not existing in experience.[3]

Every time we read a poem, we are creating a new poem—a new moment of encounter that did not previously exist. In this way, reading and criticism are also aesthetic, artistic acts.

Such acts are possible because the technology of writing presses forward into the future and demands a life beyond its moment of origination, as Psalm 102 explicitly acknowledges: "Let this be written for a later generation, / so a people not yet created might praise the Lord" (Psalm 102:18). I have noted various ways that biblical poems acknowledge this impulse toward the future, including the general openness of a good deal of prophetic poetry that signals awareness of the possibility of its own reappropriation. Another example of this futurity is in the ascriptions of psalms that attribute the poems and assign them to new uses. Consider, too, the example of several psalms with the ascription *'al-tashchet* "do not destroy,"

(Psalms 57; 58; 59; 75). "Do not destroy" is perhaps the name of an accompanying tune, though this is no longer known to us. It also reflects the theme of the psalms, which are aware of threats and seek salvation from them. We might also take it as a signal of futurity, a reinscription of the hope that underlies the impulse to write a poem in the first place, which is an act of making that resists finitude and even destruction. This is the impulse of Psalm 57. It opens with a plea for mercy and for relief from the danger of the present moment and affirms the future deliverance of the deity. Then it goes on in a moment of self-address to describe the dangers the speaker confronts: "O my soul, in the midst of man-eating lions I lie down— / their teeth are spears and arrows, / and their tongue is a sharp sword" (Psalm 57:4). In the face of dire circumstances, rather than resolving the threat, the poem moves toward its own articulation:

> My heart is firm, O God;
> my heart is firm.
> I will sing; I will chant. (Or perhaps: "I will compose; I will sing!")
> Awake, O my soul!
> Awake, O harp and lyre!
> I will wake the dawn.
> I will praise you among the peoples, O Lord.
> I will sing you among the nations. (Psalm 57:7–9)

The movement of the poem, in other words, provides a window into the poetic process, which resists the threat of obscurity with the work of making art.[4] It becomes the act that its ascriptions demands: "Do not destroy." We come to poems such as this belatedly, and to apprehend them as works of art is to see them as moments of encounter. They require an awareness of our long histories, both personal and communal, as they draw us into the sense experiences of our lives. As in our encounters with another person, they are both layered by the past, but not confined to it. Poems are always unfinished as long as they are not actually destroyed—they will remain open to new encounters as they reach forward into the future.

NOTES

Introduction

1. All translations (largely following the text of *Biblia Hebraica Stuttgartensia*) are my own unless otherwise noted. For the convenience of the reader, I employ English versification throughout, except in cases where the difference in numbering is significant, where I note both Hebrew and English. Transliterations are general purpose style, also for the convenience of the reader.
2. Fragments of Psalm 91 often appears on ancient objects and amulets. See Thomas J. Kraus, "Greek Psalm 90 (Hebrew Psalm 91)— the Most Widely Attested Text of the Bible," *Biblische Notizen* 176 (2018): 47–63; and Gerrit C. Vreugdenhil, *Psalm 91 and Demonic Menace* (Leiden: Brill, 2020), esp. 5–10.
3. Alva Noë, *Strange Tools: Art and Human Nature* (New York: Hill and Wang, 2015), xii.
4. *Against Interpretation and Other Essays* (New York: Picador, 1966), 14, 13.
5. *Against Interpretation*, 14.
6. With due respect to the ancient tradition of looking for "keys" to interpret obscure texts of Scripture, attributed for example to Sa'adia Gaon and Origen of Alexandria.

Chapter 1

1. Susan Stewart, *Poetry and the Fate of the Senses* (Chicago: University of Chicago Press, 2002), 104.
2. F. W. Dobbs-Allsopp, *On Biblical Poetry* (New York: Oxford University Press, 2015), 195–198; J. Cheryl Exum, *Song of Songs*, Old Testament Library (Louisville: Westminster John Knox, 2005); Tod Linafelt, "On Biblical Style," *St. John's Review* 54 (2012): 17–44. See also Katie Heffelfinger, *"I Am Large, I Contain Multitudes": Lyric Cohesion and Conflict in Second Isaiah*. Biblical Interpretation Series 105 (Leiden: Brill, 2011). The idea of the speaker as a hallmark of lyric itself has a history; see, e.g., Genette, *The Architext: An Introduction*, trans. Jane E. Lewin (Berkeley, Los Angeles, Oxford: University of California Press, 1992 [1979]).
3. For a helpful discussion of the historicization of the lyric "I" in classical literature, see Paul Allen Mitchell, *Lyric Texts and Lyric Consciousness: The Birth of a Genre from Archaic Greece to Augustan Rome* (London and New York: Routledge, 1994).
4. Inset poems also serve particular dimensions of the narratives themselves, as Steven Weitzman argues in *Song and Story in Biblical Narrative: The History of a Literary Convention in Ancient Israel* (Bloomington: Indiana University Press, 1997).
5. Mladen Dolar, *A Voice and Nothing More* (Cambridge, MA: MIT Press, 2006).
6. Anne Carson, *Glass, Irony, and God* (New York: New Directions, 1995), especially "The Gender of Sound," 119–142. For an incisive analysis of this phenomenon in contemporary philosophical perspective, see Kate Manne, *Down Girl: The Logic of Misogyny* (Oxford: Oxford University Press, 2018).
7. Numbers 12:1–16. For a classic discussion, see Ilana Pardes, *Countertraditions in the Bible: A Feminist Approach* (Cambridge, MA: Harvard University Press, 1992), 6–12.
8. This case is famously made by William Wordsworth in the preface to his *Lyrical Ballads* (1802).
9. The reticent dimension of biblical narrative style is forcibly articulated by Erich Auerbach, *Mimesis: The Representation of Reality in Western Literature*, New and Expanded Edition, trans. Willard R. Trask (Princeton: Princeton University Press,

2014), 3–22. Tod Linafelt has been most eloquent in addressing voice and in noting the contrasting dimensions of biblical poetic style; see, e.g., "Narrative and Poetic Art in the Book of Ruth," *Interpretation* 64 (2010): 118–129 and *The Hebrew Bible as Literature: A Very Short Introduction* (New York: Oxford University Press, 2016), esp. 69–86.

10. Seventy-three are attributed to David in the Hebrew Psalter (including the Masoretic Text on which JPS and the NRSV are based). The Greek translation (the Septuagint) attributes fourteen additional psalms to David. A psalms scroll from Qumran takes this even further, declaring that David composed 4,050 psalms. James A. Sanders, *The Psalms Scroll of Qumran Cave 11 (11QPs^a)*, *Discoveries in the Judean Desert IV* (Oxford: Clarendon, 1965), 91–93.

11. This argument has been developed by Eva Mroczek, *The Literary Imagination in Jewish Antiquity* (New York: Oxford University Press, 2016).

12. For other examples, see Psalms 57, 60, 108, and the apocryphal Psalm 151, which is the most biographical of the Davidic psalms (11QPs^a 151).

13. This is a complex phenomenon, in which the pronoun "I" may be thought of as an empty signifier that refers to and is filled by discourse itself. A classic treatment of this is Emile Benveniste, *Problems in General Linguistics*, trans. Mary Elizabeth Meek (Carol Gables, FL: University of Miami, 1971), 217–230.

14. On this point, see Carol A. Newsom, *The Self as Symbolic Space: Constructing Identity and Community at Qumran* (Atlanta: SBL Press, 2004), 215.

15. This is especially the case in the book of Psalms: though many are formulated as first-person speech, the poems are by no means monological, as Harold Fisch has observed (*Poetry with a Purpose: Biblical Poetics and Interpretation* [Bloomington: Indiana University Press, 1988], 108).

16. Carol Newsom, *The Book of Job: A Contest of Moral Imaginations* (New York: Oxford University Press, 2003).

17. See, for example, Psalms 18:13; 29:3–4; 77:17; 104:7; Job 37:2–5; 40:9. Dolar calls such instances of divine voicing "acousmatic"— their source cannot be perceived (*A Voice and Nothing More*, 62).

18. Robert Alter, *The Art of Biblical Poetry*, rev. ed. (New York: Basic Books, 2001), 141.

19. Rhiannon Graybill, *Are We Not Men? Unstable Masculinity in the Hebrew Prophets* (New York: Oxford University Press, 2016).

20. On pathos in prophetic poetry, see Abraham Joshua Heschel, *The Prophets* (New York: Harper & Row, 1962), 23–26.

21. Herbert Marks, "On Prophetic Stammering," in *The Book and the Text: The Bible and Literary Theory*, ed. Regina M. Schwartz (Cambridge, MA: Basil Blackwell, 1990), 60–80.

22. The Greek translation of the Song—for example, Codex Sinaiticus— includes rubrics that interpret sections of the Song and assign them to different speakers, making the texts all the more explicitly gendered.

23. A starting place for discussions of gender and literary voice is Hélène Cixous, "The Laugh of the Medusa," trans. Keith Cohen and Paula Cohen, *Signs* 1 (1976): 875–893. A classic discussion of women's voices is Carol Gilligan, *In a Different Voice: Psychological Theory and Women's Development* (Cambridge, MA: Harvard University Press, 1982).

24. On women's roles in ancient Israel, see Carol Meyers, *Rediscovering Eve: Ancient Israelite Women in Context* (New York: Oxford University Press, 2013). On documenting gender in oral poetries as they relate to women's lived experience, see Lila Abu-Lughod, *Veiled Sentiments: Honor and Poetry in a Bedouin Society* (Berkeley: University of California Press, 1986); and Kirin Narayan, *Everyday Creativity: Singing Goddesses in the Himalayan Foothills* (Chicago: University of Chicago Press, 2016).

25. Modesty itself has been a highly gendered category both for literary production and its critical evaluation. See the discussion in Alicia Suskin Ostriker, *Stealing the Language: The Emergence of Women's Poetry in America* (Boston: Beacon Press, 1986), 3–6.

26. A correlative to the idea of voicing is address. The idea of the suppressed audience in lyric poetry is taken up especially by Northrop Frye, *The Anatomy of Criticism* (Princeton: Princeton University Press, 1971); and helpfully problematized and historicized by Virginia Jackson, *Dickinson's Misery: A Theory of Lyric Reading* (Princeton: Princeton University Press, 2005).

27. Deryn Guest provides an overview of gender-critical readings of Jael and a Butlerian critique of the two-sex paradigm as it applies

to this text: "From Gender Reversal to Genderfuck: Reading Jael Through a Lesbian Lens," in *Bible Trouble: Queer Reading at the Boundaries of Biblical Scholarship*, ed. Teresa J. Hornsby and Ken Stone (Leiden: Brill, 2012), 26.

28. See also Ben Sira 24:3–22.

29. On this tension, see Tod Linafelt, "Private Poetry and Public Eloquence: Hearing and Overhearing David's Lament for Jonathan and Saul," *The Journal of Religion* 88 (2008): 497–526; also Steven Weitzman, "The Decipherment of Sorrow: David's Lament in 2 Samuel 1:17–27," in *Biblical Poetry and the Art of Close Reading*, ed. J. Blake Couey and Elaine T. James (Cambridge: Cambridge University Press, 2018), 257–274.

30. On the literary configuration of the emasculated male elites and the feminized land as a trope of colonial dominance, see Gale A. Yee, *Poor Banished Children of Eve: Women as Evil in the Hebrew Bible* (Minneapolis: Fortress, 2003).

31. Carleen Mandolfo, *Daughter Zion Talks Back to the Prophets: A Dialogic Theology of the Book of Lamentations* (Atlanta: Society of Biblical Literature, 2007).

32. Athalya Brenner and Fokkelien van Dijk-Hemmes, *On Gendering Texts: Female and Male Voices in the Hebrew Bible* (Leiden: Brill, 1993).

33. Naryan, *Everyday Creativity*; Alice Walker makes this point about black women's cultural productivity in her 1974 essay "In Search of Our Mothers' Gardens," in her *In Search of Our Mothers' Gardens: Womanist Prose* (New York: Open Road, 2011), 403–424.

34. I intentionally choose the feminine gendered pronoun for the speaker here. This is not a feature of the Hebrew text, but its relevance will become clear through my reading of the text.

35. On this kind of dialogue within the book of Psalms, see Carleen Mandolfo, *God in the Dock: Dialogic Tension in the Psalms of Lament*, Journal for the Study of the Old Testament Supplement Series 357 (Sheffield: Sheffield Academic, 2002).

36. For a fuller development of this reading, see Ulrike Bail, "On Gendering Laments: A Gender-Oriented Reading of the Old Testament Psalms of Lament," trans. Carrie B. Dohe, *The Writings and Later Wisdom Books*, Bible and Women 1.3, ed. Christl M. Maier and Nuria Calduch-Benages (Atlanta: Society of Biblical Literature, 2014), 179–196.

37. *The Life of Antony and the Letter to Marcellinus*, trans. Robert C. Gregg (New York: Paulist Press, 1980), 109.
38. *The Life of Antony and the Letter to Marcellinus*, 118.

Chapter 2

1. Good statements on the rhythmic features of biblical poetry can be found in several essays by Benjamin Harshav [Hrushovski], the most recent of which is "Rhythms of the Bible Revisited," in his *Three Thousand Years of Hebrew Versification: Essays in Comparative Prosody* (New Haven, CT: Yale University Press, 2014), 40–63.
2. A good place to start is David L. Petersen and Kent Harold Richards' *Interpreting Hebrew Poetry* (Minneapolis: Fortress, 1992), 21–36. For a discussion of parallelism as a linguistic phenomenon, Adele Berlin, *The Dynamics of Biblical Parallelism*, rev. ed. (Grand Rapids, MI: Eerdmans, 2008 [1985]); and M. O'Connor, *Hebrew Verse Structure* (Winona Lake, IN: Eisenbrauns, 1997 [1980]). For a thorough recent treatment of the line in biblical poetry, see F. W. Dobbs-Allsopp's chapter, "'Verse, Properly So Called': The Line in Biblical Poetry," in his book, *On Biblical Poetry* (New York: Oxford University Press, 2015), 14–94) and related bibliography. The idea of parallelism has recently been contested on linguistic grounds, e.g., Robert D. Holmstedt, "Hebrew Poetry and the Appositive Style: Parallelism, *Requiescat in Pace*," *Vetus Testamentum* 69 (2019): 617–648.
3. On perceptual, oral-aural dimensions of lines, see Emmylou Grosser, "A Cognitive Poetics Approach to the Problem of Biblical Hebrew Poetic Lineation: Perception-Oriented Lineation of David's Lament in 2 Samuel 1:19–27," *Hebrew Studies* 58 (2017): 173–197.
4. "Antithetical parallelism" is one of Bishop Robert Lowth's three categories of parallelism in his classic description of biblical poetry: *Lectures on the Sacred Poetry of the Hebrews*, trans. G. Gregory (London: S. Chadwick, 1787). One need not to reify these categories or semantic parallelism in general to appreciate the contrastive uses to which lines can be put. For vociferous and incisive critique of Lowth's paradigm, O'Connor, *Hebrew Verse Structure*, 29–54.

5. On the building impulse of parallelism, see treatments in Robert Alter, *The Art of Biblical Poetry*; and James Kugel, *The Idea of Biblical Poetry: Parallelism and Its History* (Baltimore, MD: Johns Hopkins University Press, 1981).

6. For discussion of line length in Isaiah, J. Blake Couey, *Reading the Poetry of First Isaiah: The Most Perfect Model of the Prophetic Poetry* (New York: Oxford University Press, 2015), 47–49. I assume that lines are always renegotiated in performance; see Peter Middleton, "How to Read a Reading of a Written Poem," *Oral Tradition* 20 (2005): 7–34.

7. For discussion, F. W. Dobbs-Allsopp, "The Enjambing Line in Lamentations: A Taxonomy (Part 1)," *Zeitschrift für die Alttestamentliche Wissenschaft* 113 (2001): 219–239.

Chapter 3

1. Mikhail Bakhtin, "Discourse in the Novel," in *The Dialogic Imagination: Four Essays*, ed. M. Holquist, trans. C. Emerson and M. Holquist (Austin: University of Texas Press, 1981), 293.

2. "Discourse in the Novel," 294. In invoking the Russian Formalists, I implicitly argue for formal description of artworks, not as opposed to cultural or historical or political analyses, but as their necessary condition. Others have made the case for form's ongoing necessity. Edward Said, for example, writes, "Most literary critics in Israel and the West focus on what is said in Palestinian writing, who is described what the plot and contents deliver, their sociological and political meaning. But it is *form* that should be looked at . . . the struggle to achieve form expresses the writer's efforts to construct a coherent scene . . . that might overcome the almost metaphysical impossibility of representing the present" (*After the Last Sky: Palestinian Lives* [New York: Columbia University Press, 1999 (1986)], 38).

3. Different again is Psalm 78, which uses the term *mashal* to introduce a relatively lengthy narrative poem.

4. See, e.g., *The Psalms: A Form-Critical Introduction*, trans. T. M. Horner (Philadelphia: Fortress, 1967 [1926]).

5. Later scholars have rightly been more reluctant to mine the text for earlier oral precedents. See, e.g., Marvin A. Sweeney and Ehud Ben Zvi, eds., *The Changing Face of Form Criticism for the Twenty-first Century* (Grand Rapids, MI: Eerdmans, 2003); Mark J. Boda, Michael H. Floyd, and Colin M. Toffelmire, eds., *The Book of the Twelve and the New Form Criticism* (Atlanta: Society of Biblical Literature, 2015).
6. On the complexity of the term "form," see Angela Leighton's historical overview in her book *On Form: Poetry, Aestheticism, and the Legacy of a Word* (New York: Oxford University Press, 2007), esp. 1–29.
7. Gunkel's more detailed description of the lament includes (1) summons to Yhwh; (2) complaint; (3) petition; (4) wishes against enemies; (5) affirmation; (6) protest of innocence or confession of sins; (7) acknowledgement of God's help; (8) thanksgiving or praise (Gunkel, *An Introduction to the Psalms*, 152–198). Note that Gunkel's description acknowledges considerable variation (see esp. ¶22, p. 177).
8. Chester Beatty I, group A, no. 31; Michael V. Fox, *The Song of Songs and the Ancient Egyptian Love Songs* (Madison: University of Wisconsin Press, 1985), 52.
9. Gale Yee points to a number of examples of parody, including Isaiah 1:21–22; Ezekiel 19:1–14, 26:17–18, 28:12–19, 32:2–16, 17–32; Amos 5:1–2. See "The Anatomy of Biblical Parody: The Dirge Form in 2 Samuel 1 and Isaiah 14," *Catholic Biblical Quarterly* 50 (1988): 565–586; 574, fn. 41.
10. The "Babylonian Theodicy," at 297 lines, is the longest known acrostic from ancient southwest Asia. It is conveniently available in William W. Hallo et al., eds., *The Context of Scripture Volume One: Canonical Compositions from the Biblical World* (Leiden/Boston: Brill, 2003), 492.
11. "Lecture XXIV: Of the Proverbs, or Didactic Poetry of the Hebrews," in Lowth, *Lectures on the Sacred Poetry of the Hebrews*, trans. G. Gregory (London: S. Chadwick, 1787), 275.
12. The idea that the acrostic embodies "completeness" is ancient and often remarked; see, e.g., Midrash Ruth Zuta 4:11 in S. Buber, ed., *Midrash Suta über Schir ha-Schirim, Ruth, Echah und Koheleth* (Berlin, 1894), 54. See discussion in Elie Assis, "The Alphabetic

Acrostic in the Book of Lamentations," *Catholic Biblical Quarterly* 69 (2007): 710–724.

13. Except when they're not! There is a little bit of variability, including the *pe- ayin* (ע-פ) ordering in Lamentations 2– 4 also known from inscriptions, and the omission of the *waw* (ו)-couplet and the additional *pe* (פ)- line at the ends of Psalms 25 and 34. The *nun* (נ) line of Psalm 145 is missing in MT but appears in the Psalms scroll from Qumran Cave 11, which may suggest it fell out in transmission at some point. Scholars have also noted that some biblical poems have twenty-two lines but no alphabetic head words: Lamentations 5; Numbers 23:18– 24; Psalms 33, 38, 94, 103; Isaiah 10:27–34; Sirach 6:18–37.

14. On the translation of the final lines and the openness of the ending of Lamentations, see Tod Linafelt, "The Refusal of a Conclusion in the Book of Lamentations," *Journal of Biblical Literature* 120 (2001): 340–343.

15. For further development of this observation, see Sean Burt, "'Your Torah Is My Delight': Repetition and the Poetics of Immanence in Psalm 119," *Journal of Biblical Literature* 137 (2018): 685–700; 688.

16. *Pace*, e.g., the elaborate mathematical theory of D. N. Freedman, *Psalm 119: The Exaltation of Torah* (University Park: Pennsylvania State University Press, 1998), vii.

17. Gunkel, *Introduction to the Psalms*, 20.

Chapter 4

1. Luis Alonso-Shökel writes, in rapturous language: "Images are the glory, perhaps the essence of poetry, the enchanted planet of the imagination, a limitless galaxy, ever alive and ever changing." *A Manual of Hebrew Poetics* (Rome: Editrice Pontificio Istituto Biblico, 1988), 95. To say that a verbal art is "visual" has a long history, at least as far back as Philip Sidney's 1595 claim (drawing on Aristotle) that poesy is "figuring forth . . . a speaking picture," in *A Defence of Poetry* (Oxford: Oxford University Press, 1966), 25. It is also to imply that poems and perhaps representation as such necessarily combine elements of media in diverse ways, as W. J. T. Mitchell has suggested, especially in "Beyond Comparison: Picture, Text,

and Method," in idem., *Picture Theory: Essays on Verbal and Visual Representation* (Chicago: University of Chicago Press, 1994), 83–107, though he extends his inquiry well beyond the idea of "figurative conjuring."

2. A fuller argument for this reading has been made by F. W. Dobbs-Allsopp and Elaine T. James, "The Ekphrastic Figure(s) in Song 5:10–16," *Journal of Biblical Literature* 138 (2019): 297–323.

3. Patricia Tull, "Persistent Vegetative States: People as Plants and Plants as People in Isaiah," in *The Desert Will Bloom: Poetic Visions in Isaiah*, ed. A. Joseph Everson and Hyun Chul Paul Kim (Leiden/Atlanta: Brill/SBL, 2009), 17–34.

4. In modern literary studies the language of "signifier" and "signified" comes from Ferdinand de Saussure's influential *Course in General Linguistics* (New York: McGraw Hill, 1966). The language of "source" and "target" is used in cognitive linguistics and conceptual metaphor theory, introduced by George Lakoff and Mark Johnson, *Metaphors We Live By* (Chicago: University of Chicago Press, 1980). For a discussion of the history of metaphor theory, and a discussion of simile as metaphorical see Janet Martin Soskice, *Metaphor and Religious Language* (Oxford: Clarendon, 1985). For an overview of specific metaphors in the Hebrew Bible, see Pierre van Hecke, ed., *Metaphor in the Hebrew Bible* (Leuven: Leuven University Press, 2005).

5. I use the term "more-than-human" following David Abram, *The Spell of the Sensuous: Perception and Language in a More-Than-Human World* (New York: Vintage Books, 1996).

6. Terence E. Fretheim, *God and World in the Old Testament: A Relational Theology of Creation* (Nashville: Abingdon Press, 2005), esp. 249–268.

7. This is a central concern of earlier presentations of biblical poetry, as in Johann Gottfried Herder's "Dialogue III," in *The Spirit of Hebrew Poetry*, vol. 1, trans. James Marsh (Burlington: Edward Smith, 1833). More recently, such views have been discussed, e.g., by Mari Joerstad, *The Hebrew Bible and Environmental Ethics: Humans, Non-Humans, and the Living Landscape* (Cambridge: Cambridge University Press, 2019).

8. William P. Brown, *Seeing the Psalms: A Theology of Metaphor* (Louisville: Westminster John Knox, 2002).

9. Jennifer Metten Pantoja, *The Metaphor of the Divine as Planter of the People: Stinking Grapes or Pleasant Planting?* (Leiden: Brill, 2014).

10. Feminist readings have often made this point. See, e.g., Johanna W. H. Van Wijk-Bos, *Reimagining God: The Case for Scriptural Diversity* (Louisville, KY: Westminster John Knox, 1995); Janet Martin Soskice, *The Kindness of God: Metaphor, Gender, and Religious Language* (Oxford: Oxford University Press, 2008).

11. L. Juliana Claassens, "Rupturing God-language: The Metaphor of God as Midwife in Psalm 22," in *Engaging the Bible in a Gendered World: An Introduction to Feminist Biblical Interpretation*, ed. Linda Day and Carolyn Pressler (Louisville, KY: Westminster John Knox, 2006), 166–175.

12. For discussion of Isaiah's gendered metaphors, see Hanne Løland, *Silent or Salient Gender? The Interpretation of Gendered God-language in the Hebrew Bible, Exemplified in Isaiah 42, 46, and 49* (Tübingen: Mohr Siebeck, 2008).

13. The sense of the text's excess of meaning is implicit in rabbinic interpretation's four types of exegesis (sometimes referred to with the acronym *Pardes: Peshat, Remez, Derash*, and *Sod*) and in ancient Christian interpretation's fourfold senses of Scripture (literal, allegorical, tropological, anagogical).

14. A helpful resource for understanding how the artistic context of the ancient Near East can illuminate biblical texts is Othmar Keel, *The Symbolism of the Biblical World: Ancient Near Eastern Iconography and the Book of Psalms*, trans. Timothy J. Hallett (New York: Crossroads, 1985). For a theoretical statement on visual hermeneutics and the importance of iconographic exegesis, see Ryan P. Bonfiglio, *Reading Images, Seeing Texts: Toward a Visual Hermeneutics for Biblical Studies*, Orbis Biblicus et Orientalis 280 (Göttingen: Vandenhoeck & Ruprecht, 2016).

15. For a discussion of this translation and a fuller exploration of the poem, see Elaine T. James, "'Silence Is Praise': Art and Knowledge in Psalm 65," in *Biblical Poetry and the Art of Close Reading*, ed. J. Blake Couey and Elaine T. James (New York: Cambridge University Press, 2018), 32–48.

16. "On the Art of the Future," in idem., *The Open Studio: Essays on Art and Aesthetics* (Chicago: University of Chicago Press, 2005), 17.

17. *The Works of St. Augustine: Expositions of the Psalms, 99–120*, trans. Maria Boulding (Hyde Park, NY: New City Press, 2001), 101; *The Works of St. Augustine: Expositions of the Psalms, 51–72*, trans. Maria Boulding (Hyde Park, NY: New City Press, 2001), 323.

Chapter 5

1. Paul Ricoeur, *The Conflict of Interpretations* (Evanston, IL: Northwestern University Press, 1974).
2. *Interpretation Theory: Discourse and the Surplus of Meaning* (Fort Worth: Texas Christian University Press, 1976), 30–31.
3. See Steven Weitzman, "Text and Context in Biblical Studies: A Brief History of a Troubled Relationship," in *The Wiley Blackwell Companion to Ancient Israel*, ed. Susan Niditch (London: John Wiley & Sons, 2016), 67–83.
4. On "memory" as a productive category for historical inquiry, see Daniel Pioske, *Memory in a Time of Prose: Studies in Epistemology, Hebrew Scribalism, and the Biblical Past* (Oxford: Oxford University Press, 2018).
5. For an account of the undetermination of texts and a theory of biblical reception "contexts," see Brennan W. Breed, *Nomadic Text: A Theory of Biblical Reception History* (Bloomington: Indiana University Press, 2014), esp. "Anchor or Spandrel: The Concept of the Original Context," 75–92.
6. I am not drawing strong distinctions here between allusion, quotation, and other varieties of intertextual relationships. My definition draws on G. Brooke Lester, *Daniel Evokes Isaiah: Allusive Characterization of Foreign Rule in the Hebrew-Aramaic Book of Daniel* (London: Bloomsbury, 2015), 4–9; 13. For two significant treatments of biblical allusion, see Michael Fishbane, *Biblical Interpretation in Ancient Israel* (Oxford: Clarendon, 1985); and Richard Hays, *Echoes of Scripture in the Letters of Paul* (New Haven, CT: Yale University Press, 1989).
7. James A. Sanders, *The Psalms Scroll of Qumran Cave 11, 11QPs.a Discoveries in the Judean Desert of Jordan 4* (Oxford: Clarendon, 1965), 91–93. David is also explicitly called a prophet in Acts 2:20.

8. See, for example, the discussion in Hans Wildberger, *Isaiah: A Commentary* (Minneapolis: Fortress, 1991), 271–272.

9. Yvonne Sherwood argues that this is especially the case for the prophetic poetry. See "'Darke Texts Needs Notes': On Prophetic Prophecy, John Donne, and the Baroque," *Journal for the Study of Old Testament* 27 (2002): 47–74. Stephen A. Geller writes, "This creative indeterminacy is clearly not accidental or incidental." See "The Riddle of Prophecy," in his *Sacred Enigmas: Literary Religion in the Hebrew Bible* (London: Routledge, 1996), 137.

10. See Craig A. Evans, *To See and Not Perceive: Isaiah 6:9–10 in Early Jewish and Christian Interpretation* (Sheffield: Sheffield Academic Press, 1989).

11. John F. A. Sawyer, *The Fifth Gospel: Isaiah in the History of Christianity* (Cambridge: Cambridge University Press, 1996), 100–125.

12. For a thoughtful account of how the Bible has been shaped by trauma, see David M. Carr, *Holy Resilience: The Bible's Traumatic Origins* (New Haven, CT: Yale University Press, 2014); on this point, see "Jerusalem's Destruction and Babylonian Exile," 67–90.

13. On the complexities of victim-blaming, see Christopher Frechette, "The Old Testament as Controlled Substance: How Insights from Trauma Studies Reveal Healing Capacities in Potentially Harmful Texts," *Interpretation* 69 (2015): 20–34.

14. The text of the decree, the famous "Cyrus Cylinder," is widely available. See, e.g., *Context of Scripture 2* (Leiden: Brill, 2003), 315.

15. On this point, see Ricoeur, *Interpretation Theory*, 79.

16. Sadler also points to how Psalm 137 has been a resource for many different contemporary groups who have struggled for survival. Rodney S. Sadler Jr., "Singing A Subversive Song: Psalm 137 and 'Colored Pompey,'" in *The Oxford Handbook of the Psalms*, ed. William P. Brown (New York: Oxford University Press, 2014), 447–458.

17. Douglass writes, "I am no minister of malice. I would not strike the fallen. I would not repel the repentant, but may my right hand forget its cunning, and my tongue cleave to the roof of my mouth, if I forget the difference between the parties to that terrible, protracted and bloody conflict." Frederick Douglass, "To

Unknown Loyal Dead, speech delivered at Arlington National Cemetery, Virginia, on Decoration Day, May 30, 1871," *Frederick Douglass: Selected Speeches and Writings*, ed. Philip S. Foner and Yuval Taylor, The Library of Black America (Chicago: Lawrence Hill Books, 1999), 609.

18. James Weldon Johnson, ed., *The Book of American Negro Poetry* (New York: Harcourt, Brace, 1922), 36–38. See also James Cone, "The Recrucified Christ in Black Literary Imagination," in his book *The Cross and the Lynching Tree* (Maryknoll, NY: Orbis Books, 2011), 93–119. I am grateful to Blake Couey for the reference and discussion.

19. These lines appear in the version published in his collection *Felon* (New York: W. W. Norton, 2019). An earlier version in *Poetry* (April 2016) does not include these lines, https:// www.poetryfoundation.org/poetrymagazine/poems/88739/ when-i-think-of-tamir-rice-while-driving.

20. "The Other America," (1967–68), Civil Rights Movement Archive, https://www.crmvet.org/docs/otheram.htm. Audre Lorde writes, "Anger is an appropriate reaction to racist attitudes, as is fury when the actions arising from those attitudes do not change. . . It is not the anger of other women that will destroy us, but our refusals to stand still, to listen to its rhythms, to learn within it, to move beyond the manner of presentation to the substance, to tap that anger as an important source of empowerment." "The Uses of Anger," *Women's Studies Quarterly* 9 (1981): 7–10.

21. Babylonian Talmud, *Gittin*, 57b. Discussed in James Kugel, *In Potiphar's House: The Interpretive Life of Biblical Texts* (Cambridge, MA: Harvard University Press, 1994), 175.

22. There are many other examples of later re-appropriations of this text, including the famous Rastafari song "Rivers of Babylon," by the Melodians (1970), from another context in which former slaves of African dissent decry political oppression. See Nathaniel Samuel Murrell, David T. Shannon, and David T. Adamo, "Psalms," in *The Africana Bible: Reading Israel's Scriptures from Africa and the African Diaspora*, ed. Randal Bailey et al. (Minneapolis: Fortress, 2010), 225. For discussion and overview of interpretive traditions, see Susan Gillingham, "The Reception of Psalm 137 in Jewish and Christian Traditions," in *Jewish and Christian Approaches*

to the Psalms: Conflict and Convergence, ed. Susan Gillingham (Oxford: Oxford University Press, 2013), 62–82; 71.

23. See, also Psalms 76; 84; 87; 122. Hermann Gunkel, *An Introduction to the Psalms: The Genres of the Religious Lyric of Israel*, trans. James D. Nogalski (Macon, GA: Mercer University Press, 1998), 29; 55–56.

24. As others have noted, the psalm's canonical context—its placement within the larger structure of the book of Psalms—is also a significant literary context. See, for example, Nancy deClaissé-Walford, *The Shape and Shaping of the Book of Psalms: The Current State of Scholarship* (Atlanta: SBL Press, 2014). Yair Zakovitch notes that Psalm 137 "interrupts" the close relationship between 136 and 138, but its proximity to 136 and 138 enable hope in God's past deliverance and promise of future justice ("On the Ordering of Psalms as Demonstrated by Psalms 136–150," in *The Oxford Handbook of the Psalms* [New York: Oxford University Press, 2014], 214–228; 216).

25. Left-handedness is viewed as exceptional in the ancient world, and the iconography of scribes in ancient art regularly depict the scribe with stylus in the right hand. Note the close association between text and mouth in Ezekiel 2:8–3:11; the tongue is associated with poetry in 2 Samuel 23:2; Isaiah 28:11; 50:4; Psalm 35:28; 39:3; 51:14; 119:172. These formulations blend oral/aural performance with the literate convention of writing. We see a similar overlap in Psalm 45:1: "My tongue is the pen of a quick scribe."

26. Though it does not include a superscription indicating so, it bears some resemblances to the psalms of Asaph, a figure associated with temple ritual and with the songs of Zion (esp. Psalms 73–83). See Frank Lothar Hossfeld and Erich Zenger, *Psalms* 3, trans. Linda M. Maloney (Minneapolis: Augsburg Fortress, 2011), 514.

27. See also Deuteronomy 32:25; Hosea 13:16 [Heb. 14:1]; Isaiah 13:15–18; 2 Kings 8:12; Jeremiah 51:20–23.

28. Translated by William Holladay, *The Psalms Through Three Thousand Years* (Minneapolis: Fortress, 1993), 172; from Germain Morin, *S. Hieronymi Presbyteri Commentarioli in Psalmos* (Turnhout: Brepolis, 1959), 165–242.

29. *The Works of St. Augustine: Expositions of the Psalms, 51–72*, trans. Maria Boulding (Hyde Park, NY: New City Press, 2001), 240.

30. This can be seen amply in hymns and liturgical texts. See Jonathan Magonet, "Psalm 137: Unlikely Liturgy or Partisan Poem? A Response to Sue Gillingham," *Jewish and Christian Approaches to the Psalms*, 83–88; and Joel LeMon, "Violence Against Children and Girls in the Reception History of Psalm 137," *Journal of Religion and Violence* 4 (2016): 317–335.

31. William H. Bellinger, Jr. "Psalm 137: Memory and Poetry," *Horizons in Biblical Theology* 27 (2007): 5–20; 17.

32. James Longenbach, *The Resistance to Poetry* (Chicago: University of Chicago Press, 2004), 97.

Conclusion

1. The term "New Criticism" comes from John Crowe Ransom's *The New Criticism* (Norfolk, CT: New Directions, 1941).

2. Robert Alter, *The Art of Biblical Poetry*, rev. ed. (New York: Basic Books, 2001).

3. John Dewey, *Art as Experience* (New York: Penguin, 1934), 113.

4. For a theory of ancient art as participating in eternity, see Zainab Bahrani, *The Infinite Image: Art, Time, and the Aesthetic Dimension in Antiquity* (London: Reaktion Books, 2014).

INDEX

For Biblical entries with chapter and verse numbers, page numbers follow the biblical reference after a space.